novum pro

AF161517

Brigitte Hoffmann-List

Jean-Pierre de Smet

Missionary of the Indians
Beloved by all

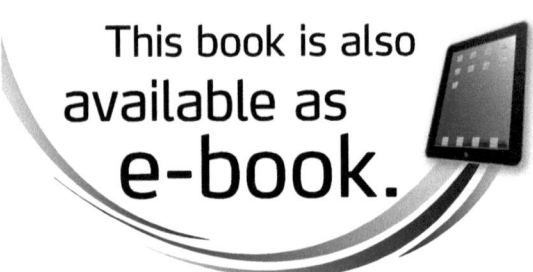

© 2025 novum publishing gmbh
Rathausgasse 73, A-7311 Neckenmarkt
office@novumpublishing.com

ISBN 978-3-7116-0217-6
Editing: Kirstie Stuart-Hieß
Cover photo: Getty Images
Cover design, layout & typesetting:
novum publishing
Internal illustrations: Getty Images

The images provided by the author have
been printed in the highest possible quality.

All rights of distribution, including via film, radio, and television, photomechanical reproduction, audio storage media, electronic data storage media, and the reprinting of portions of text, are reserved.

www.novumpublishing.com

*Dedicated to my secret advisor,
Laura Ingalls-Wilder,
from DE SMET in South Dakota.*

Contents

A Call in the Night 9
Problems with the Indians 19
Captured by Indians 25
The Release 33
Visits to the Neighbors 37
Happy Days 41
New Settlers 57
The Council of Laramie 61
The Murder of Marshal Tom Smith 68
Sheriffs and Gunslingers 74
Prayers – Christian and Heathen 77
Encounter with the Indians 79
The Meeting with Sitting Bull 83
A Community Forms 90
Epilogue 94

A Call in the Night

They had just sat down to supper. The wind was howling and hissing around the house, but it could not get inside. The wind and the cold were stuck outside. Ma stood and put another log into the oven. Inside, it was cozy and warm, but outside, it seemed to Kathie, all hell had been unleashed.

Suddenly, they heard a noise that stood out from the sounds of the wind. It sounded like a call and the snort of a horse. Susan, the little black cat, hid herself away in the farthest corner of the room. Pa stood up, grabbed his rifle, and opened the door. At first, they couldn't see anything in the blackness and the swirling snow flurries, and the new arrival probably felt the same way because he stared into the room as if he first had to remember where he was.

"Come in, come in!" said Pa, pulling the stranger into the room and closing the door behind him. The man leaned against the wooden wall and took a deep breath:

"Praise be to Jesus!"

"Forever and ever, amen!" said Ma, and helped him to a chair. "Please, take off your coat, I will dry it by the fire."

"Yes, thank you," said the man, listlessly, and unbuttoned his thick coat made from buffalo hide. Around his neck he wore a ribbon with a silver crucifix hanging from it.

"De Smet!" Pa cried out, surprised. "Father De Smet!"

"How do you know who I am?" asked De Smet.

"Your crucifix, of course; and I have seen you before as well."

"Where?" asked De Smet.

"In Oswego."

"Oh, my goodness – Lizette!" shouted De Smet and jumped up. "I can't leave the poor animal outside in the cold! Would you happen to have some room in your stable?"

"Of course! We have one horse and one cow, there is surely room for a third animal, too." They both went out into the night with the roaring storm and returned a few minutes later.

"So, now Lizette is taken care of, just like me," he said thankfully. "You cannot imagine how happy I was to come across a house with light shining through the cracks! An inhabited house! My journey was supposed to end in Independence, but it is another 14 miles to ride."

Ma brought hot tea with brown sugar and quickly made some sandwiches filled with cold game. "Please, strengthen yourself," she said, "and drink some tea. You must be half-frozen!" He took a couple of sips and then said:

"Ah, that feels good! I am finally beginning to thaw out!"

Kathie looked at his strangely beautiful face, his brown hair that hung down to his shoulders, and his shining eyes that kept gliding over the family as he eagerly ate his snack.

"It has been a long time since I have had something this good to eat!" he confessed.

"It is fresh game," said Ma. "My husband shot it just a few days ago."

"You probably don't get to eat regularly on your travels, do you?" said Ma.

"No, not usually. But I always have some provisions with me, and when I pass by an Indian village, they are always very welcoming. You are invited to eat, and the more you eat, the more they like you. It would be an insult not to eat, but they do not pester you to do so. Anything you cannot finish, you may take with you. Once I was invited to eat with a family. They placed a dish in front of me, and it looked like some disgusting kind of broth. I had to steel myself to try it. And then – I was quite astounded, how good it tasted! It was a stew made of buffalo tongue with herbs and potatoes."

De Smet had finished his meal and looked at the family hopefully. He wanted to learn more about them and their circumstances.

"Don't the Indians get in your way when you are hunting?" he asked.

"No," said Pa, "at least, not until now."

"You must be very brave, to settle here ..."

"We have neighbors," said Pa, "three families, with whom we have good contact. We are secretly hoping that a town will grow up here, with a church, a school, a little store …"

"This is Indian country," said De Smet.

"The land belongs to whoever builds on it," Ma argued, "that is just common sense!"

"Well, it is not quite as simple as that," said De Smet gently. "The Indians have been living here for centuries. The land feeds them. They live from hunting and fishing. The buffalo gives them everything that they need. Furs for their clothing. Leather for their tepees, meat – everything, really. And they only kill as much as they need. When the whites invade here, they kill everything out of sheer hunting lust. And, of course, with the ulterior motive of depriving the Indians of their livelihood."

"How can we solve this problem?" asked Pa. "What do you think?"

"I think about it day and night, but I don't know either. But there is a faint glimmer of hope, for me, when the Indians send their children to school. There they learn to read and write. They learn everything about working the land, the different working techniques and maybe, one day, they can be integrated into the United States. That is the only way to save them. That would be humane and just. I hope and pray that that will come to pass one day. I often imagine how this fertile land will be populated. Here, there is everything that the farmer needs. Farms with orchards, herds of sheep, cattle, …"

"And a lot of chickens," reminded Kathie, who loved chickens above all.

"Chickens, of course!" De Smet smiled at her. "Towns will grow up, the farmers will provide them with everything. But what about my Indians? Will they be able to keep up? I am so afraid that they will be driven from the land where their fathers and forefathers were buried."

They were all silent for a while. Each one lost in their own thoughts.

Then De Smet spoke once more:

"The most wonderful thing I ever heard on this subject was from an Indian. His name is Red Jacket."

"The Indians give speeches?" asked Ma, surprised.

"Yes," said De Smet, "and they have a very poetic way of expressing themselves. May I repeat the speech to you, as far as I can remember it?"

"Please do," said Pa.

"There was a time when our forefathers owned this great island. Their feats extended from the rising to the setting of the sun. The Great Spirit had made it for the use of the Indians. He had created the buffalo, the deer, and other animals for food. He had made the bear and the beaver. Their skins served us for clothing. He had scattered them over the country and taught us how to take them. He had caused the earth to produce corn for bread. All this he had done for his red children because he loved them. But an evil day came upon us. The white man came. Their numbers were small. They asked for a small seat. We took pity on them, we granted their request, and they sat down among us. We gave them corn and meat. In return, they gave us poison – fire water. The white people had now found our country. More and more came amongst us. Yet we did not fear them. We took them to be friends. At length, their numbers had greatly increased. They wanted more land; they wanted our country.

You have now become a great people, and we have scarcely a place to spread our blankets. You have got our country but are not satisfied; you want to force your religion upon us.

We understand that your religion is written in a book. If this was intended for us as well as you, why has not the Great Spirit given it to us? How shall we know when to believe, being so often deceived by the white people? – You say there is but one way to worship and serve the Great Spirit. If there is but one religion, why do you white people differ so much about it?

We also have a religion, which was given to our forefathers, and has been handed down to us, their children. We never quarrel about religion. – The Great Spirit has made us all, but he has made a great difference between his white and red children. Since he has made so great a difference in some things, why may we not conclude that he has given us a different religion according to our understanding? The Great Spirit does right. He knows what is best for his children.

We do not wish to destroy your religion or take it from you. We only want to enjoy our own."

"How wonderful!" whispered Kathie.

"Yes, it is wonderful," said Father De Smet, "but it is aimed directly at me. In plain language it means: we do not want your religion."

He leaned back and closed his eyes. It had grown dark in the room, only the fire still burned and threw shadows up the walls. Ma and Pa were also moved.

"I can't believe that this text came from an Indian," said Ma. "When I think of the Indians, I just think of the atrocities that they commit."

"Because they have no other choice," said De Smet, "they take revenge on the whites who keep taking everything away from them."

Once again, everyone fell silent.

Then De Smet said "But I have seen a lot of good things, too. A great deal of interest in our religion. When I come into a village, I am often welcomed with a little speech; for example, the chief will say: 'Speak, Black Robe! We are all your children. Show us the path we are to follow, to get to the place where the Great Spirit lives. Our ears are open. Our hearts will follow your words!' Whenever I hear such a thing, I am, of course, happy. I speak to them about the mission, and I ask them to give up their wandering life. I teach them the profession of our faith, the Lord's Prayer, Hail Mary, and the 10 Commandments. And we sing a lot together; the Indians in their language, and me in Latin. It works very well. The joy of spending time together prevails."

"Oh, I should love to see it one time!" said Kathie quietly. Ma's eyes widened with shock.

"Well, maybe you can one day," said De Smet seriously, "the nearest mission is only around one hundred miles away."

"Can they accept our religious truths?" asked Ma.

"Only in part. They are passionate gamblers, for example. They risk everything. 'Thou shalt not covet thy neighbor's goods' is something they don't understand. On the other hand, they are very generous. What's mine is yours too. If they have ceded a piece of land to the government, they don't realize that they have lost it."

"Then how will it all work?" asked Pa.

"I don't know," said De Smet glumly. "But I trust in God's help. He sent me here. There were only twelve apostles, who accomplished the conversion of the whole world."

"Do they listen, when you tell them about our religious truths?" asked Ma.

"Yes," he said. "They love the stories from our Holy Scripture, of the Creation, the Flood, Noah's Ark. I often sit with them in the meadow and tell them all about it. Those are wonderful times."

"And is it successful? Do they believe it?"

"They like the stories. I don't know how much of it they accept. Their medicine man is very important to them, of course, with his superstitious practices. I don't know who is stronger. What's more, the whites don't set a very good example. They are lied to and deceived. And they should adopt their religion? But what I do know for sure is that they love and appreciate me, and they believe me. It's all a very big, very complicated business." He let his head fall into his hands.

"Do you believe that the salvation of souls can only be achieved through the Roman Catholic religion?" asked Pa.

"Yes," said De Smet with conviction, "yes, I believe that."

"But you also like the Indian religion, don't you?" asked Pa.

"Yes," said De Smet, "I like it. It is beautiful. It appeals to me. It is like a beautiful picture, a beautiful painting. But God's son came down from Heaven to help us, to save us! They do not believe in that. And in the Holy Mass we can be with Him, unite with Him, through wine and bread. – My desire and my goal is the salvation of souls! They must learn about our faith!"

"And if they don't learn about it?" asked Kathie.

"But I am here; I must tell them!"

"And if you don't?" insisted Kathie. "Our God is good and merciful; he will not leave them in the dark after their death just because they have not experienced the light!"

"There are similarities with our religion," said De Smet finally, "they believe in a Creator, the Fall of Man, the Flood, and a divine mediator who speaks to the 'Lord of Life' on their behalf. And the poetry contained in the religion of the Indians always fascinates me. They say that everything the power of the world does is in the form of a circle. The sky is round, and the earth is round too. The wind develops its greatest power in vortices. Birds build their nests in circles. The sun rises and sets in a circle. Just like the moon, and they are both round. Even the seasons form a circle in their cycles and always return to where they were before. Human life is a circle from childhood to childhood. And so, it is with everything in which the 'Force' stirs."

"That is beautiful," said Kathie.

"Yes, it is," said Ma, "one cannot imagine that people who are so cruel can have such thoughts."

"The whites are crueler than them," said De Smet quietly, "they take everything that they need to survive from them."

Everyone was silent for a while.

"And what part of this 'Indian wisdom' did you like best, Kathie?" asked De Smet finally.

"The part about the birds that build their nests in a circle because they have the same religion as humans," said Kathie. He looked at her and his eyes twinkled a little.

"Me too. I also know another poem by a child: 'Who tells the tree when the time has come to grow its leaves? Who tells the thrush that it is now warm, and they can once again fly north? Birds and trees listen to something that is wiser than they themselves. They would never know it on their own.'"

"I am speechless," said Ma.

"So am I," said Pa.

"One cannot get enough of listening to you!"

"I am pleased to hear that," said De Smet and smiled a little, "and that's why I want to tell you something that can make us laugh!"

"Yes, please!" Kathie was delighted. "We shall all laugh together now! We haven't done that yet."

"That is true. Humor should not be neglected. We all love to laugh. So, here is the story. Several weeks ago, I was in a camp of the Crow Indians on the Yellowstone River. I was given a friendly welcome. I stayed there for a few days, and their hospitality was very tiring for me. On one day, I had to take part in 20 meals. I had to do it, but I used the time to tell them about our religion. I told them about our 10 Commandments. The Indians listened carefully, but they were astounded at what I was telling them. In the end, the chief exclaimed: 'I think – well, the way I see it – there are at most two in our tribe who won't go to hell! These are the only two that I know of who have neither killed nor stolen. But if they have, then it's clear that we're all going to hell together!'"

Pa laughed, until the tears ran down his cheeks, but Ma asked, what was there to laugh about. De Smet, who had also looked on with amusement, immediately became serious.

"You are right, there is not really much to laugh about. But I had to anyway. They say everything so freely. It's so refreshing and happy to be with them. And you know exactly where you are with them. They do not pretend."

"Neither do we," said Kathie.

"No, of course not. I didn't mean it that way. But they are no match for the subtleties of the whites who negotiate treaties with them and then twist them around so that the Indians get the short end of the stick."

"You mean the wrong, devious thing?" asked Kathie.

"Yes, that's what I mean," said De Smet, "and there should be some truth in what is proposed to the Indians."

"Yes," admitted Pa. "And that is why the Indians have so much confidence in you, because you are fundamentally different from the other whites. I once heard it said that De Smet is the only white man who doesn't speak 'with a forked tongue'."

"I am certainly not the only one," said De Smet, "but they are bitter. That is why they speak so."

By now, it had become late.

"Time for bed!" said Ma and looked at Kathie. But Kathie couldn't take her eyes off the handsome man sitting in the corner, his head leaning against the wall, his face half-lit by the firelight.

"Will you be able to sleep, Father?" she asked quietly.

"Certainly!" De Smet beamed. "How do you think I have been sleeping in the past few weeks? Alone, in the forest, in the snow, huddled in my coat, with my travel bag as my pillow."

"Wasn't it awfully cold?" asked Kathie.

"No," said De Smet, "buffalo skins keep you very warm."

"And you weren't afraid?"

"No. Of what then? I am in God's hands. And the noises I could hear were good for me: the rustling in the trees, the hooting of an owl, the distant howling of the wolves."

"But what if they come closer?"

"They don't. And if they did: it is in God's hands."

"Father, would you like to say a prayer with us before we all go to sleep?" asked Ma.

"With pleasure," said De Smet and stood up. The others stood as well. Ma smoothed out her apron and Kathie hurried to adjust the sleeves of her dress, which had become a little too short for her.

"The Lord is my shepherd," he said with his warm, beautiful voice, "I shall not want, he makes me lie down in green pastures, he leads me beside quiet waters. Even though I walk through the valley of the shadow of death, I will fear no evil, for you are with me." He stretched his hand out in order to bless them.

"And please think of the poor Indians," said Kathie quietly.

"Now I would like to say an Indian poem: 'The day is coming to an end. Think again about the worries it has brought you. Keep a few of them, throw the others away!'"

Then Kathie climbed up the wooden ladder to the loft, Ma would follow soon. The two men remained by the fire, which was now only glowing. The wind howled around the house, but couldn't get in. Pa had built the wooden cabin too well.

The next morning, when they came down, De Smet was no longer there. He had ridden away in the early hours of dawn. It was a long ride to Independence. They ate their breakfast in silence.

"I didn't get a chance to say goodbye," said Kathie quietly. The food stuck in her throat. Later she helped Ma to wash the breakfast crockery and to clean the house. Suddenly, she ran to Pa, who stood in the doorway looking out, and threw her arms around him tightly. "He will come back, won't he?"

"Yes," said Pa and hugged her to him.

"He will. He belongs to us in a tiny way, didn't you feel it too?"

"Yes, I felt it, but he belongs to his missions, his Indians …"

"He also belongs to us," said Pa with certainty, "and that is why he'll come back."

Problems with the Indians

Spring came in all its glory; the prairie turned into a sea of flowers. The flowers bloomed in all possible colors. Birds soared high and swooped down to earth like arrows. The prairie dogs came out of their dens, and prairie chickens crisscrossed their paths. On the nearby pond, ducks cavorted, and the sky was blue with white clouds floating by like sailing boats.

The White family, who had settled here the previous spring, lived in the hollow. Mrs. White had become a dear friend to Ma. She had two daughters, both younger than Kathie, with whom she liked to play. They cut out paper dolls and dressed them, they played ball or tried their hand at chess, but one child always had to watch, and so they moved on to joint activities such as temple hopping or word games. Mrs. White had been a teacher back east and tutored her children, and Kathie was welcome to join them. She often read to them from the Bible, and Kathie was certainly the best at reciting the psalms; but there were also lessons in literature, history, and the sciences.

Ma didn't mind it if she visited the White family often. A narrow path led straight from their house into the prairie and then dipped down. It went around the hill and there, in a hollow, was the White's house. It couldn't be seen from Kathie's house, as tucked away as it was. It was larger and more impressive than Kathie's house, had a stable and large gardens round the house, but she still liked her own house better.

Alongside the house ran a path that led down to the river. And this led to an Indian village on the banks of the river. The children were never allowed to continue down this path. The danger was too great.

This path was an Indian path. Mr. White had told them that once, he had thought the path had been abandoned, given up by the Indians. But it wasn't. It happened very often that Indians rode along the path. They did it in their own proud way, without paying any attention to the people standing there staring at them. Mrs. White always hurried back into the house. She was very afraid of the Indians. And Mr. White had once said that he would never have built the house here, if he had known that the Indians still used this path.

One time, they had even entered the house. Billie, the younger daughter, said that her Ma had nearly had a heart attack. It was two Indians, who had commanded her Ma to cook something. Half dead with fear, she complied with this wish and fried up some eggs and bacon, which the Indians devoured greedily. Then they searched the kitchen and the pantry for more food and took everything that they could carry.

"They were hungry," noted Kathie.

"And that is a reason to enter our home?"

"We are on their land," said Kathie, "and that is why they consider everything on it to be their property."

"This is our land," said Billie, "we have settled here!"

"Yes, you settled here," said Kathie, "and so did we. But the ground on which we have done this belongs to the Indians."

"How do you know that?" asked Billie.

"From De Smet, from Father De Smet, our friend. He explained everything to us. He knows everything. He has good contact with the government. And he has good contacts with the Indians. He knows all about it."

"De Smet?" asked Helen, the older sister, who had come nearer. "Who is that then?"

"A Jesuit priest; a missionary, who lives in St. Louis. But he travels through the land and visits the Indian tribes. He is very much admired by them. Most of them, at least; but there are tribes, who have an indelible hatred of all white people because they have done so much to them. And he is, after all, a white man."

"Will we also get to see him one time?" Billie asked curiously.

"Yes, maybe," said Kathie. "He will come to visit with us this year, in summer. At least, that is what he promised."

In May, the wild roses bloomed, and the pond was full of life. Kathie helped Ma in the house, they tended their small garden and took care of the animals in the stable. The chickens ran around clucking, the horse and the cow were in the stable, but were sometimes allowed out, to graze on the fresh green grass. Pa liked to lock them in in the evening. It had happened more often recently that voices could be heard coming from the river where the Indians lived, louder than usual. Sometimes you could also hear drums.

Pa and Ma didn't know what that meant, and there was nobody they could ask. There was danger in the air.

"Why don't you have a dog?" Billie asked one time, when Kathie was over for a visit. They had a large, black dog called Prince, who protected the whole family. Even when Kathie came, who he knew, bared his teeth and was sometimes hard to calm.

"We had a dog," said Kathie, "he was also really wild, but we loved him a great deal. But there were some problems with the Indians."

"Why?" asked Billie.

"Our dog liked to circle the house when Pa was gone. He really was our protector. Sometimes, when Pa was in Independence, getting some things at the store, he ran for miles to meet him. But then it happened that he encountered Indians on the path that led past our house and wouldn't let them pass. In his eyes, it was Pa's path, and not the Indian's. One day, one of the Indians stopped – just as Ma came out of the house – and lifted his shotgun and took aim at our dog. Ma was able to call the dog into the house, but we all knew what would happen as a result. One day, a nice couple came by in a covered wagon with children and some animals. They stayed with us for a night and the man told Pa that he was looking for a good guard dog. So, with a heavy heart, Pa gave our Bob to the immigrants. We were all very sad but agreed with Pa's decision. The family was friendly and he was given a good home. If he had stayed with us, he would have been shot by an Indian at some point."

"That is a sad story," said Billie.

"Yes, it is," said Kathie. "But it has a happy ending. The family was very nice and loved animals. He will have a good life. His future here would have been that one day we would have found him dead on the Indian trail. That would probably have been the worst thing for all of us. He was such a good dog. He deserved to get a second chance, and he got one."

"It's still a sad story," said Helen, who had joined them. Her eyes were moist. "But how do you protect yourselves, then? After all, we live in Indian country! Our parents always reassure us, but I actually believe that we know where we stand. We're not so small anymore that we don't understand how things are. We are living dangerously. We are in enemy country."

"No," said Billie. "This is our land. Our parents built on it, so it belongs to us."

"No," Kathie disagreed, "this is not our land. It is Indian country. Whether we build on it or not, it does not belong to us. It belongs to the Indians. This land may one day become settler land, but it is not that yet."

The children fell silent.

"Do our parents know that?" asked Billie.

"I don't know," said Kathie, "probably not. But they hope that we can stay. Here in the prairie, so close to a river, the earth is fertile, the sky is wide open – it looks like there's room for everyone!"

"It looks like that," said Helen, "but we'll have to wait and see whether the Indians allow it."

June came along, the grass stood high, and it was fun to hide in it. Prairie chickens crossed the path with their young, and sometimes Kathie had the feeling that she was being watched. But that was probably only due to the tall grass that obscured her view.

Once, at lunchtime, she told Pa about all the animals that crossed the path and then disappeared again to the tall grass.

"That's nice," said Pa, "let's just hope that it isn't something else that crosses your path one day."

Kathie was astounded.

"What do you mean?" Ma gave Pa a reproachful look. Pa returned her look and said.

"Indians". And then he said to Ma:

"She is old enough, she should hear about it now."

"Why do you say that?" Kathie asked breathlessly.

"Something is not right with the Indians," said Pa. "You know that I often go down to the river to chop wood. And it has often happened to me that I have met an Indian. We greeted each other in a friendly way, and each went on his way. Last week, I met another. He stopped a way away, lifted his rifle and took aim at me. It was just like the time that an Indian took aim at our dog. It was a warning. He meant to say: not one step further, you are in my country now. The wood that you chop belongs to me."

"What did you do?" asked Kathie.

"I turned around, and I left." Ma sighed.

"What should we do?"

"I don't know," said Pa. "But for now, we will wait."

Captured by Indians

One day, as Kathie was walking in front of the house – she didn't dare to go far away from it – she saw a tall figure on a horse coming towards her. The prairie grass had already grown so high that it closed over him immediately. She stood spellbound. The rider stopped and dismounted.

"De Smet!" shouted Kathie and ran towards him.

"Kathie!" He lifted her up and swung her around a few times, before carefully setting her down again.

"Father De Smet, oh what good fortune! Please come inside and visit with us, we have been so worried!"

"First, I must see to Lizette, do you want to help me do that?"

"Yes," said Kathie and stroked her gently. "She is such a beautiful horse!"

"It is a mule," said De Smet, "sure-footed, loyal, and devoted. I wouldn't exchange her for any other animal." Lizette observed Kathie with her intelligent eyes and flicked her long ears.

"She likes me!" said Kathie, thrilled.

"That's no wonder," said De Smet gently. They went to the stable and tied her to a chain. They gave her water and a small bowl of corn.

"Will you stay the night with us?" said Kathie, anxiously.

"Oh yes," said De Smet, "if I may."

They entered the house. Ma jumped up from where she had been making a fire.

"Oh Father," she said, "what a surprise! I was just fixing lunch. My husband will be here in a few minutes! Will you eat with us?"

"Gladly," said De Smet. He sat on the bench near the window and Kathie sat down next to him. Ma cut thin slices of bacon and lay them in a pan. Once they had browned, she added eggs and laid potato slices on top. That was lunch.

In the meantime, Pa had come home and was surprised to find De Smet there.

"What a pleasure," he said, "and what a wonderful act of providence! There are some things I want to ask you. We have been very worried here."

"John, please wait until Father De Smet has finished eating," Ma requested, "we can't just start pestering him with our business as soon as he walks in the door. – Please, help yourself!" Everyone put something on their plate and ate with a hearty appetite.

"Finally, a home-cooked meal!" he said. "My provisions this time were somewhat meager. A little bread, some dried meat, and cold potatoes."

"If I had known that we would be having a visitor, I would have baked a cake," said Ma.

"Oh, I am sorry to miss that," he said, smiling.

"And you, Kathie, can you cook as well?"

"Yes," said Ma, "she can cook anything. But she is an especially good baker." Kathie looked at Ma gratefully. "Her speciality is apple pie!"

"Apple pie?" wondered De Smet. "Where do you get apples from around here?"

"They are dried apples," said Kathie. "Pa brings them sometimes from Independence. But the pie tastes just as good with pumpkin! We grow those here."

"Do you often have visitors?" asked De Smet.

"No, not any more. We used to visit each other often, to help each other. There are four families here nearby. Now we don't dare to wander too far from our houses."

"What has changed compared to how it used to be?"

"The Indians. We used to think they would accept us, but we don't think that any more. They also used to come by, mainly to get something to eat and also to steal something on the side; that was part of it. Now we haven't seen any Indians for weeks. You can hear drumming and shouting from the bottom of the valley at night. It's as if two groups are fighting."

"Two groups?" asked De Smet attentively. "What Indians are they?" Ma's eyes widened. For her, Indians were Indians; all equally ugly, all equally smelly, all equally cheeky.

"I think they're Osages," Pa said hesitantly.

"It would be good to know who the others are," said De Smet. "If they are Sioux, the situation could become dangerous. The Sioux have sworn to kill any white man who falls into their hands."

"But why?" asked Ma. "We want to live here peacefully; we won't hurt them. Couldn't you expect them to behave in the same way?"

"The Sioux have already been through too much with the whites. Moved on again and again, starved again and again, the Indian agents cheat them through and through. So, it's not surprising that they don't want to see any more white people. I've heard that they kill every white man, no matter who it is and whether he has done them any harm or not."

The adults fell silent. But Kathie spoke up: "I could sneak up and see what's going on. I'm small, and when it's dark I can get very close to them. I can make observations and then share them with you. I can be helpful!"

"You cannot be serious!" said Ma appalled. "Even if you could get all the way to their camp – which of course we would never allow you to do – you would have little chance of understanding the situation. Imagine a bunch of quarrelling Indians! You wouldn't understand what they're saying, you don't know the language!"

"I can tell the difference," Kathie insisted, "between one group of Indians who are at odds with each other and two different groups. I think I have the confidence to do that."

"And I wouldn't put it past you to wish it and want to do it, but it would be downright madness to try. You're a brave girl, Kathie, but now I don't want to hear any more about it."

"Maybe I could try it," De Smet said slowly. "I may not be so small and delicate that I could meander through the grass as invisibly as our Kathie, but it might be possible under the cover of darkness."

He thought about it. "I'd have to take off my cassock, otherwise I won't be able to sneak up on them." He laughed a little. "On the other hand, it could protect me. But I'm not traveling as a missionary now, I want to know what is spoken so that the settlers can follow it."

"Do you understand the Osage language?" asked Pa.

"Yes," said De Smet, "but not that of the Sioux. But in this case it doesn't matter. They will behave in such a way that I can gather what I want from their conversations."

"I don't want you to go, Father," said Kathie quietly.

"Is that so? You want to go but you would not let me go?" He looked at her with amusement.

"I could have better excuses," Kathie said. "I could say I got lost; I'm just a kid; that doesn't carry as much weight."

"Children have been taken, too," De Smet said seriously. "And then, years later, they were found somewhere. It's not a game."

Kathie had to admit defeat. So, they all sat together on the bench in front of the house, each lost in their own thoughts.

Pa told De Smet, how far they had all come here, how happy they were living here, and that one day a village would be built here, with a church, a school and stores that would meet the settlers' daily needs. The open sky, the wide plains, the nearby river – it was all so perfect for a settlement!

"But it is still Indian land," said De Smet gently. "It does not belong to the whites. And the Indians will fight for it."

"Couldn't we all live here together – in peace?"

"That would be nice, but I don't really believe it. The land that the whites are settling on, has been given to them. It is 'Indian Territory', and they will fight for it. The more white people come, the more land is taken away from them. They can't cope with that. Some tribes – or parts of some tribes – have come to terms with the whites. They cede their land and receive payments in return. But they are not treated fairly. They are lied to and cheated. They don't receive what was promised. Then they have to move on. They try this and that, stay near the forts and missions that offer them protection, cultivate fields, give up again, move on. They are a nomadic people by nature. Their happiness lies in hunting, in war games, in riding. They are not farmers."

"And their religion?"

"Is beautiful. They worship nature. God is in everything, in every human being, every animal and every blade of grass."

"You want to take it away from them?"

"No. God created nature. It is good to believe in it and to worship it. I just want to convey to them that Almighty God, the Creator God, has set a sign and sent His Son – a part of Him – to earth. When we celebrate the 'Great Prayer' – the Holy Mass – He is in their midst; they can turn to Him as a person with all their worries. He listens to them and sends them His angels. This is union and the highest happiness. Union with the Creator God. And this faith promises eternal life."

In the meantime, dusk had fallen, a light wind was blowing, and the sounds of the evening birds could be heard. Ma stood up to usher everyone into the house, when suddenly the sound of muffled drums could be heard from afar. Ma stood rooted to the spot.

"Not again!" she whispered. Pa stood up and put an arm around her shoulder reassuringly.

"Come now, we are used to that by now," he said, "there's no need for that to scare us anymore. And what's more, we have Father De Smet here with us today, he can protect us."

"I don't think so," said De Smet, "because I am leaving now." Ma and Pa looked at each other in dismay.

"I'm going to sneak down there, and sound out the situation."

"No," shouted Kathie.

"Quiet, child!" he said and embraced her slightly. "I have to know what I am dealing with. If everything goes well, I will come back and report to you. If there is danger, you will have to be careful or maybe even leave the area. If this is just a peaceful meeting between two tribes, then I will find that out, too."

"And if they capture you?"

"We are all in God's hands," said De Smet, shortly.

He went to the barn to check on Lizette. Kathie watched as he removed his cassock and stuffed in into his travel bag.

He removed his crucifix that hung on a leather band. Kathie saw that he held it in his hand briefly, as if he were unsure whether he should keep it or leave it here. Then he came back and placed it in Kathie's hand.

"Take care of this for me," he said, "and when I come back, you can give it back to me." Kathie held it tightly in both hands. She looked at him as he stood before her, in his robe made from thin brown leather, he had taken his shoes off.

"I will be quieter without shoes," he said and smiled a little.

"I know," said Kathie flatly. And in the blink of an eye, he had disappeared into the darkness.

Kathie went back into the house. She hid the crucifix in her apron pocket. She didn't really know why she couldn't tell her parents what he had given her. It seemed like a bequest to her. He hadn't given it to Pa or Ma, but to her.

All three sat in the parlor and watched as the fire in the hearth slowly died. Ma lit the petrol lamp. The flame cast a warm, bright light. No-one spoke. Then Pa said:

"He's not taking that big a risk. He knows the Indians and the Indians know him. If he really were to be discovered – I think, he would have a good chance."

"But what if the second group – if there even is one – is vicious and bloodthirsty? He is still a white man!"

"It could also be," said Kathie, "that the Indians don't know him. Who knows what groups have come together down there!"

"You could be right," Pa agreed.

For a long time, they sat together, nobody wanted to go to bed. Susan, the black cat, came from her comfortable place near the chimney and sat in Kathie's lap. It was almost as if she wanted to be a part of it and share the family's worries. Kathie stroked her soft fur thoughtlessly.

Outside it had grown silent; like the calm before the storm. Ma's hands, which were otherwise always busy with sewing or knitting, lay in her lap. Pa smoked his pipe and stared at nothing. Occasionally, he would look over to the door, next to where his rifle hung. Finally, he stood and pulled the leather strap that served to bar the door, inside. Now no-one could enter from outside.

"Time for bed!" he said cheerfully. That meant that Kathie should go up to her room. "Tomorrow is another day!"

At that moment, a terrible howling and screaming arose from the bottom of the valley and Kathie rushed to the door.

"Stay here!" Ma shouted in a voice that Kathie had never heard from her before.

"They have him," Pa said quietly, "they've captured him."

"Do you think they've killed him?" Kathie whispered.

"No," said Pa, "that scream was the sign that they have made a capture that is important to them. They'll find out who he is and maybe exchange him for Indian prisoners or try some other kind of blackmail. If they had killed him, they would have done it quietly. A stab, a scalping, and then thrown him in the bushes somewhere. No, I'm sure that he is still alive. And if they think he is an important prisoner, then he will be well treated. That much I know about the Indian ways."

"Come now, child," said Ma and put her arm around Kathie's shoulders. "There's nothing we can do for him now. He is a strong, brave man. He speaks the Osage language. God will help him. He puts so much trust in Him." Kathie turned and began to climb the stairs.

"Take Susan with you. She'll comfort you." Susan crept behind her.

Upstairs, she crawled into bed and pulled her rough covers over her. She took the crucifix from her apron pocket and held it tightly in both hands. She lay like that for a while, staring at the small window. The night-black sky with the stars looked threatening. She usually loved the dark night and the stars that surrounded her, but that had all changed today.

Downstairs she could hear Ma and Pa talking to each other quietly. After a while it fell silent. A light wind buffeted the house. This evening had been so nice, the four of them by the fire or in front of the house.

The Release

She suddenly realized that she was still wearing her dress; she had forgotten to put her nightgown on. And she also realized that she couldn't stay there. She stood up and hid the crucifix in her apron pocket once again. She took some sheets from the basket and knotted them together. Then she attached the whole thing to the edge of the window and carefully lowered herself down. She had to jump the last bit. Then she walked quietly to the stable. Lizette was tied up outside and looked at her with wide eyes.

"Be very quiet!" she whispered as she put the crucifix in his traveling bag. "We're going to go get your master now." The clever animal seemed to understand her and snorted quietly.

Kathie climbed on her back and took up the reins.

"We are going to go towards the river! It's not far at all!" She rode along the Indian path near her house and then dropped down into the hollow of the valley. After two miles she came to a small pond, where there was a solitary dog rose bush. Kathie dismounted and tied Lizette up.

"You won't have to wait very long," she whispered.

She bravely crept through the tall grasses. It went steadily downhill and soon she heard a rushing sound. It was the river. Suddenly she smelled a fire and saw a faint light between the tree trunks. It was the Indian camp. Now she crawled closer on all fours, for it was possible that the Indians had set up a guard that might spot her. Suddenly she could make out a large, black mass in front of her. It was a tent. It stood apart from the other tents, which stood out dimly in the faint light. An Indian was sitting in front of the tent. He was playing with a small pipe hanging from a leather strap around his neck. A murmur could be heard in the distance.

The Indians were still talking.

Was this tent, standing so far away, the tent where prisoners were kept? And was the Indian there the guard?

She crept so close that she bumped her head against the tent wall. Then she lifted the fabric a little to look inside. That's when she saw him.

He was sitting down, tied to a stake with his back to her.

She didn't hesitate for a moment. It was too good a chance to miss. She grabbed his hands, which were tied together behind the beam, and cut the strap in two with the small knife she always carried with her. She had expected De Smet to make a quick move, but that was not the case. He remained as still as before. He waited.

"Lizette is at the pond with the dog rose bush," she whispered almost silently. A small movement of his body told her that he had understood her. Then she slowly and carefully withdrew again.

She crept back along the first stretch; first on the ground, then upright, turning around again and again; but no one followed her. The last stretch she ran as if a pack of wolves were after her, and she was happy when the night-black cottage appeared in front of her. How glad she was to be home again, to know Pa and Ma and Susan were there. How nice to have a home, safety!

She knocked at the front door. The door was pulled open, and Pa stepped out, gun in hand. He looked at her in astonishment. Now she felt her knees go weak, but her father caught her and carried her into the room. There he sat her down in the rocking chair.

"Where were you?" Pa and Ma were horrified.

"I set him free!" she whispered, as a tear slowly made its way down her cheek.

"Where, in Heaven's name, have you been?"

"At the bottom of the valley with the Indians."

"No – it can't be true."

"It is. And it was not even hard. Nobody saw me."

"Do you even know what you risked?"

"Yes. My life. But he is also risking his for us. And his risk is greater than mine. I'm still a child."

Then came a short confession; she said everything that was necessary, and got a long hug from Ma, who didn't want to let go at all.

"May I stay down here with you?" she mumbled. After all the excitement she suddenly felt so weak that she no longer wanted to go up the stairs at all.

"You stay here with us," said Pa and lifted her up. He gently laid her down on the large bed and said: "Sleep now. We are here with you." Ma turned the petrol lamp down low and slid under the blanket next to her. Pa laid down on her other side. She lay there between them, safe and sound. She was just falling asleep when she suddenly remembered something and laughed quietly to herself.

"What's wrong?" Ma asked, worried. "Are you alright?"

"Yes," said Kathie, but I just had to think about all three of us lying in bed fully dressed!" Now Pa had to laugh, too.

"We decided to do this today to be prepared for an emergency."

"Me too," said Kathie.

The next morning, Kathie went up to close the window. Ma followed. She gathered the knotted sheets back in through the window and looked over at Kathie. Kathie looked back at her.

"I had to do it, and I think you know that, too," she said quietly. Ma nodded. Then she untied the sheets and packed them back into the chest. Kathie stayed upstairs for a while and waited until Ma called her to breakfast. She heard her parents talking quietly downstairs.

"She could have broken her neck!"

"She could have, but she didn't," said Pa. "She is something special! She is superior to us all."

Visits to the Neighbors

The next few days passed like a dream for Kathie. She did all her work mechanically and felt a great sense of satisfaction. She went into the barn and milked the cow. She fed the chickens and helped in the fields. She harvested carrots, potatoes, and turnips and stored them in the shed. She had a warm, good feeling. That was her work. She was at home.

Now and then, Pa left to shoot something, so they had fresh meat. Sometimes a rabbit, sometimes a pheasant. There were ducks at the pond.

Nothing more was heard of the Indians. Nor did the settlers dare to go too close to the valley floor or hunt in the forest.

Now and then, Pa would ride into Independence, to run errands and purchase whatever the family needed at Irwin's Store. It was a meeting place for settlers and fur traders from all directions; news was exchanged, and games were also played, but Pa never took part.

The summer passed and fall came to the country. Since that night, Kathie had always wondered if and how he had managed to get out of the tent and get to his horse. Back then – the next day – she had been eager to go to the pond and see if Lizette was still tied up. But it would have been madness to try. After all, her parents never left her unobserved for a moment. Secretly, however, she knew that he had succeeded.

Now that things had settled down with the Indians, Ma allowed Kathie to visit the White family again. The first time she came along because she wanted to talk to Mrs. White about the state of things.

They sat around the large table in Mrs. White's bright, friendly kitchen. Mrs. White served tea and small cakes. Helen und Billie had also come to fortify themselves. Then they wanted to start with their lessons. Mrs. White had already set out some books and paper for the children.

"How do you like all of this?" asked Ma.

"Not at all," said Mrs. White. "Of course we can live here somehow. We can get up in the morning, make the beds, prepare breakfast, tidy up, cook, eat, work in the garden, go to bed. That would be our life. We could visit our neighbors in danger. That would be all. There's not much more we can do. I feel like a mouse in a trap here."

"How would you like to live then?" asked Ma.

"With the prospect of improvement. With the prospect of something. A small community, a few houses, a church, a store, a small school perhaps. What will happen to our children? Where will they get an education?"

"You can give them that," said Ma. "You know so much. You're almost like a scholar."

"It's still not enough," said Mrs. White. "A school awards certificates. I can't do that. And with such a certificate, a child can continue their education, go to a higher school, specialize, gain specialist knowledge."

"De Smet builds schools like that," Kathie said quietly.

"Yes, but for Indians, not for us," said Mr. White, who had just come through the door. He hung his rifle up behind the door and sat down heavily on a chair.

"Nothing to shoot?" asked Mrs. White, worriedly.

"Nothing," Mr. White confirmed grimly. "It's almost as if the Indians have taken all the damned game with them."

"But Tom!" said Mrs. White, reproachfully.

"The other day I went to the pond to shoot a duck, but there were no ducks there either. Then I saw the big dog rose bush – Kathie felt a stab to her heart – and there was a rabbit sitting under it! As soon as I raised my gun, it had disappeared. So, this one also got the better of me! But, knowing you, we still won't have to go hungry!"

"No," said Mrs. White cheerfully, "this evening there'll be beans and salted meat, and I've baked some fresh bread, too. And there's enough for everyone."

Late in the afternoon, Ma and Kathie made their way home because they wanted to be home before dusk. They didn't have to wait long, because as soon as it was dark, they heard Pa's cart. He led the horse into the stable and then came in whistling happily.

"Look at my treasures!" he called out. He brought flour, brown sugar, tea, dried apple slices, pickles, beans, salted meat, and small, sweet cakes. They put everything on the table and marveled at these delicacies.

"And the best thing," he called out, "news from De Smet!" Kathie held her breath.

"What is it?" she groaned.

"He was involved in a brawl; in Oswego."

"It can't be true!" Ma had to sit down. "I may believe a lot, but I can't believe that!"

"Believe it!" said Pa. "I have it on good authority. Mr. Irwin's brother was in a saloon there –"

"In a saloon?"

"Yes," said Pa and smiled, "and De Smet was there too."

"But a saloon is a place where people drink and gamble and where there are loose women, and that's where De Smet is supposed to have been?"

"He must have had his reasons," said Kathie.

"Yes, he did. A fight broke out there, with De Smet beating the living daylights out of one of the men and then dragging him out into the street."

"But why, for heaven's sake? A Catholic missionary? What kind of behavior is that?"

"Obviously there was no other way," said Pa. "The other guy was an Indian agent. He was known to cheat the Indians again and again, making promises and breaking them, giving them food that was inedible and chasing away women and children who were hungry. De Smet taught him a lesson that he will remember and that will get around. De Smet has many friends who help him." Kathie could no longer hear what the adults were saying and discussing. The voices merged into noises that became louder or softer, and a single thought animated her: he was alive! He was alive!

Happy Days

It was another three years before they saw him again. Kathie was just feeding the chickens when she saw – just like last time – a tall figure riding towards her. She dropped the bowl and stared at him. He drew closer and closer until he pulled up in front of her and jumped down from his horse.

"Oh, Father!" she said almost silently. He came towards her and took her hand. Then he pushed her away a little to get a good look at her.

"Kathie!" he exclaimed. "You have grown into a beautiful young lady!"

"No," said Kathie, "I haven't. I am still your child." After he had taken care of Lizette, they entered the house together. He sat down on the bench where he had last sat, and she sat opposite him.

"That was very daring, Kathie, back then," he said seriously, looking at her.

"No, I don't think it was." And then: "I just had to do it. I had no other choice."

"Still, it was very brave," he said, "you don't know what Indians are capable of when alcohol is involved. They act like madmen and slaughter everything in their path, even their own children."

"Was alcohol involved?" asked Kathie.

"No," said De Smet, "otherwise I probably wouldn't be here now."

In the meantime, Pa and Ma, who had been working in the field, had come in, and their joy at seeing De Smet was great.

"Where have you come from this time, Father?" asked Pa, as he was shaking hand heartily.

"From Independence," said De Smet. "But I wanted to make a short stopover here before I ride back to St. Louis. You know I have my reasons."

"Yes," said Ma gently.

"And where were you before that?"

"In the Rocky Mountains."

"What?" Pa shouted. "That's not possible!"

"Yes, it is," said De Smet, laughing, "all in all it was 4000 miles, and I think I managed them well."

"But not with Lizette?"

"No, of course not. I had her stabled in Independence. There's a livery stable behind Irwin's Grocery and she did well there. Independence has become quite a town, by the way. It has everything you could wish for: Houses, gardens, a church, a school, a doctor, a farrier, a saddle maker, a shoe store, a furniture store, a fashion store, a bakery, and of course the old-established merchant. I think the school would be interesting for the girls one day …"

"I would like to think so too," said Ma sadly, "but we're stuck here. We can't move. If a neighbor makes his field just a little bit bigger, it is devastated in a short time; if someone builds a shed somewhere, it is soon burned down; as if by magic. It happens somehow invisibly; nobody sees Indians going or coming. It's as if they want to tell us: 'Stay where you are and don't move. We won't hurt you, but you mustn't get any bigger either'".

De Smet looked very serious.

"They won't do anything to you, because if they were going to, they would have done it already."

For a long time, nobody said anything, then De Smet asked:

"What would you have imagined?"

"A small, independent community," said Ma, "church, school, a store, the great big sky above us, the rolling prairie under our feet. Good contact with others; joie de vivre. But that probably doesn't exist; at least not here for us."

"It does exist elsewhere," said Pa, "I hear a lot at my meetings in Independence. A lot of small communities are springing up and, with a bit of luck, they're growing. Trading posts are opening up, they attract a lot of people, they're building railways nearby …"

"Which brings us back to my point," said De Smet. "This is Indian country, allocated to the Indians by the government, after they have been displaced countless times, so, if I know anything, they won't want to give up even a hand's breadth of it. If the railway project near here does come about, they would fight that vehemently and with everything at their disposal. And they have a lot at their disposal."

"I know what you mean, Father," Kathie said quietly. "But what should we do?"

"I don't know either," said De Smet. "The law is the law. And the land belongs to them. Simple as that."

"But I know what you should do now, Father," Ma said energetically. "You must eat! What must you think of us! What a bad hostess I am!" She hurried to the hearth, cut some potatoes and meat into the skillet, and fried everything off until it was crispy. She added some small, pickled cucumbers to the side of the plate.

"Please! Eat! It is all for you; we have eaten already!"

"Yes, I am really hungry," De Smet admitted, and ate what Ma had set in front of him, with a great appetite.

"It's clear that you haven't been getting anything good to eat recently, Father," said Ma, smiling.

"Is it that noticeable? It's true! I have only been eating moss recently."

"Moss?" Kathie was amazed. "What do you mean? You can't eat moss!"

"You can! It is a plant that grows close to the ground in small pillows. It is full of vitamins. And it is edible. An Indian showed me."

"And how does it taste?"

"Absolutely terrible. It tastes just as awful as it looks. But it can save your life. I never would have dared to bite into it if the Indian hadn't told me about it. There are many poisonous plants, of course. I am very interested in plants; I have a small herbarium. It is a great joy of mine and relaxes me. The Indians, who are so connected with nature, help me with it. It is something we have in common, God's Creations, it is for everyone. All children are equal under God's creation."

He stood up. "I have to take a walk outside," he said.

"Of course," said Pa, "it's such a beautiful day!" Everyone could tell that he needed a few minutes to himself.

He walked towards the stable and sat down under the small tree that Pa had planted there. He looked down towards the river, above which the treetops loomed in shadow. He sat like that for a while, gazing into the distance. Then he lay down, his arms crossed behind his head. He was surely watching the great white clouds, drifting by like ships. He might even have nodded off. And who could blame him.

In the meantime, Ma and Kathie watched the dishes and cleaned the kitchen up. Pa sat in the window seat and smoked his pipe.

"He must be exhausted," said Ma.

"Oh, I don't think so," said Pa, "he has the constitution of an ox. From what I have heard tell from folks, he's pretty much invincible. People are afraid of him. He is hard and sharp towards his opponents, who are, of course the opponents of the Indians, and generous and amiable towards all who are of good will and support his friends, the Indians."

"Do you think he will tell us where he's been these past three years? All that he has experienced?"

"Yes, perhaps," said Kathie, "but we shouldn't press him."

After a short while, he came back inside, looking fresh and rested.

"A cup of tea?" asked Ma. "I just made a fresh pot!"

"Yes," said De Smet, "that would be lovely." Ma poured him a cup, which he took thankfully.

"I bet it's been a while since you had one," said Pa.

"Yes, it's been quite a while. Sometimes, when we are camped near a fort, they give us tea, coffee and sometimes even chocolate. But that doesn't happen often. And sometimes, when we're riding through the forests or rough country, there's no opportunity to make anything. Often, we see a trail and don't know who could have made it. It could be enemy scouts watching us. Of course, that makes us a little uncomfortable. So, we ride on, without turning around. If there are enemy scouts behind us, then they can't know that we are suspicious. We find a campsite and light a large campfire. We sit around the fire and let it burn down. In the darkness, we sneak over to our horses, mount them and ride away as quietly as we can, and as fast as we can. We ride for half the night until we find a suitable hiding spot. Then we dismount, wrap ourselves in our blankets and fall straight to sleep. There is never time to make a cup of tea!" He smiled to himself a little in his usual way.

"When you camp in the forest, do you hear animal noises?" asked Kathie.

"Yes, of course!" said De Smet. "You hear owls, bears growling, the call of a puma, the howling of wolves."

"And you're never afraid?" asked Ma, who had sat down alongside them with her knitting.

"No," said De Smet, "we are all in God's hands. And the sounds of the forest are pleasant to me."

"But the Indian trails are unsettling to you?" asked Pa.

"Yes," said De Smet, "but mostly because of my companions. There are Indian tribes who have sworn to kill the first white person that they meet. That could also be me. It is hard to see the difference between friend and foe in the darkness. It almost happened once already. The Crow that wanted to attack me saw my crucifix and recognized at the very last moment."

"Oh, Father!" he called, "do you realize how close you came to eternity!"

"That was close," said Pa. "Weren't you afraid?"

"No," said De Smet, "I am not afraid. They know me and know that I am well-disposed toward them. But there is another tribe: the Sioux. Their hatred for the whites has grown so great that they have sworn to kill every white man they meet. You have to come to terms with that; it could happen.

One time we were attacked by Sioux, who had been trailing us for a while. They wore warpaint and were armed with rifles, bows, and arrows. They galloped up to us. I stood fast and showed them my cross. I held it up high. The Indians pulled up. A Canadian, who was with me and who spoke a little Sioux, told them: "This man speaks with the Great Spirit. He comes to visit the different Indian tribes." And the Indians laid down their weapons. Each of them shook my hand. I gave each of them a little tobacco; they like that. Then they sat down in a circle around me and smoked the peace pipe. Sometimes –" here he stopped talking and smirked a little, "I have to try very hard to remain serious. I tend to laugh; and that is a most holy act. Sometimes I have these really strange, frayed figures sitting around me, with this strange warpaint, and pass their pipe around with a deadly serious expression. I have to suppress my laughter, otherwise I'd fare badly. Well, the chief invited me to spend the night in his village."

"But they were Sioux?" asked Pa.

"Yes, but there are different groups, the 'good' and the 'bad'. Whereby the bad are not bad, they have just lost faith in the white people. They only want revenge and to kill."

"And this group were the 'good' guys?"

"Yes. The aggressive ones, the so-called Yanktonnais – Sioux, live beyond the Missouri. They are led by the famous chief Sitting Bull. – Now, they accompanied me into their village and offered me a place of honor in the chief's tent. Surrounded by forty warriors, he said: "Black Robe, this is the happiest day in our lives, because for the first time we have a man in our midst who is close to God. I invite you to a great feast that is being prepared for you."

There was a really huge feast with great big hunks of roasted bear, and we ate, smoked, talked, and sang till late in the night, and I was pleased to be able to withdraw to my tent when everything quietened down at around midnight. I was just drifting off to sleep when I noticed a glint of light. I saw that the chief had entered the tent and had a knife in his hand."

"No!" Ma gasped, horrified.

"Yes. The candlelight had fallen on the steel of the blade; that was what I had seen. He held the knife to my chest –"

"Oh no, please no!" said Kathie, almost soundlessly.

"Nothing happened, I am here, after all," said De Smet reassuringly.

"He said: 'Black Robe, are you afraid?' I took the chief's hand, placed it upon my chest and said: 'Feel, does my heart beat faster than usual? Why should I be afraid? We have smoked the peace pipe together, I have eaten with you, and I am as safe here in your tent as I am in the house of my father."

"That was very brave," Pa said seriously.

"Not at all," said De Smet, "if you know the Indians and their code of honor. The chief just wanted to test whether I really trusted him."

De Smet had finished his tea and now rose.

"The day is still young," he said. "I am not used to sitting around doing nothing for so long. Doesn't anyone have any work for me? Surely there is always work on a farm!"

He and Pa went outside. Through the window, Kathie saw them heading towards the barn. Pa was surely showing him the animals. Then he showed him his fields, a cornfield, a wheat field, and a field of beets. There was also potatoes, pumpkins, tomatoes, and beans. Later, Kathie heard chopping and sawing, and in the evening Pa told them that De Smet had helped him to repair the fence and improve the stables.

"He is unbelievably strong!" Pa said to Ma when he came back in again. De Smet had stayed outside with the animals.

"He lifted a heavy wooden beam as if it were kindling. I could really use a neighbor like him!" He washed up in the washbowl behind the door and dried himself.

"Fix us something good to eat!" he said to Ma. "He'll be hungry."

De Smet came in shortly afterwards.

"Time for supper!" said Ma, "I have made a bean soup. Do you like bean soup?"

"Yes, I do," said De Smet, "bean soup is one of my favorites!"

"Mine, too," said Kathi, beaming.

"We could eat outside," said Pa, "now that the weather is so nice. And it is still light."

"Sure," said De Smet. He and Pa sat on the bench in front of the house, while Ma warmed the soup and Kathie cut fresh bread that she had baked that morning. The sound of the men's chatter and the smoke from Pa's pipe drifted through the door. Of course, the men were talking about the current situation. Pa told his side; that they would all pull together, but that nobody really knew what to do and everyone was simply living from one day to the next.

Then Ma and Kathie brought the food, and everybody ate heartily except Kathie, who could not tear her eyes away from De Smet. She was so happy to have him here. A good friend for her Pa, her Ma, and for her, too! What could be better!

In the meantime, night was falling and there were fireflies in the air, and every now and then a dark bird would swoop down onto the prairie.

"What an atmosphere!" said Pa. "Kathie, please, bring me my harmonica!"

Kathie rushed to bring it. It was Pa's greatest treasure, in a green leather case, and had accompanied him on all his travels. He took it out and checked the pitch. And then he began to play: "In the morning the birds sang, the flowers bloomed and there was sunshine everywhere, even in my mood." Ma and Kathie joined in, but then Ma said:

"This doesn't suit at all, John! Can't you play something else?" They all had to laugh. He played another couple of faster tunes, and Ma and Kathie sang along, as best as they could. And then he played one long note, and everyone sang happily:

> *"Should auld acquaintance be forgot*
> *and never brought to mind?*
> *Should auld acquaintance be forgot,*
> *and days of auld lang syne?"*

De Smet raised his voice and joined in at this point. He had a soft, warm voice, which struck Kathie to her very heart. They both stopped singing and just hummed, so that they could hear the sound of his voice. It rose up and mixed with the glitter of the stars. Kathie was happy. She wished that this evening could last forever. She thought of all the songs about the old days. This day was now. It could not be earlier or later. It was now. And they were all together.

The next day Pa and De Smet went to work in the fields. Then they worked in the stable. Later they came in and Ma had set out a good breakfast.

"Pancakes!" shouted De Smet. "I haven't eaten these in such a long time!" Ma set a plate in front of each of them and poured maple syrup over them. Then there was toasted bread with cranberry jelly that Ma had made in the fall.

Later they went back to the fields and worked until the early evening. Kathie heard sawing, banging, and chopping and she knew, that they were repairing all manner of things. There was always plenty to do on a farm.

Finally, they both came in. Kathie had laid the table particularly nicely and placed a vase of prairie flowers in the middle. She had spread out a tablecloth and there were also napkins. Knives, forks, and spoons were set out and along came Ma and filled the bowls with steaming hot soup. There was also bread, butter, cheese, and fresh lettuce from the garden.

"Well, you got me beat as far as farmwork is concerned," Pa said after the meal, leaning back comfortable and lighting his pipe.

"Oh, no," said De Smet, "certainly not. Why do you say that?"

"You just notice everything. And you are so skilled!"

"Necessity has taught me that," said De Smet. "There were three of us when we arrived in St. Louis, and we had absolutely *nothing*. We had to build our own huts, furnish them ourselves, cook for ourselves, darn our own clothes, we only had ourselves. We had no help. That is the reason that I can do a little bit of everything. If you want to help others, you must first learn to help yourself."

"But you always kept your greatest task ahead of you and that made you strong," said Ma.

"Yes," said De Smet, "you are right. Our main task is, and has always been, to save souls. But our beginnings were humble, deplorable. We often had to hold mass in huts that had no roofs, where the congregation were exposed to wind and weather. In winter, the snow would cover the altar, and in summer the wax candles melted. We had to endure all this and keep sight of our main goal."

"Of course, your main concern was for the whites?" asked Pa.

"Yes, of course. Many lived in lonely settlements, ten, twenty miles apart. We had to search for them; and it was often dangerous. Sometimes we spent the night in the middle of the forest, surrounded by the howling of wolves, we had to cross rivers on horseback, or sometimes in a canoe. But we have all always enjoyed good health.

Gradually, however, I became aware of how the Indians were feeling. Robbed of their land, pushed farther and farther out west by the whites, they found support and refuge in the Catholic Church. Time and again groups arrived and asked for a Catholic priest.

So that is why we built the first mission. That was St. Joseph's Mission for the Potawatomi Indians. And it was a success.

And then we founded the St. Mary's Mission, among the Salish Indians. They live a nomadic life, and it was difficult to keep them in one spot. I wrote to the government often, asking them to help me to keep them together in villages, to teach them agriculture, give them tools, animals, and seeds."

"Was that difficult?" asked Pa.

"Yes," admitted De Smet, "very difficult. For both sides. The Indians love their free life; they become restless and unhappy if they have to stay in the same place for too long. And it didn't work out from the other side, either. They never received the things that had been promised to them. I can only ask, not demand. I have no power."

"Yes, you do," said Ma, "you have power. You are known. And you move in government circles. You will be listened to. "

"They listen to me," De Smet said slowly. "And I am promised a lot. But there is a big gap between theory and practice."

"Do you have plans?" asked Pa.

"Yes," said De Smet, "I do. I want to help my Indians. I want to see them happy. But now something else has been brought to my attention by the government, and I don't know how to behave. Gold has been found in the Black Hills, which has resulted in an onslaught of the whites into the Indian territories. The Superintendent of Indian Affairs is now planning a council at Fort Laramie, where the Indians are to receive compensation for the land that the whites have taken away from them to build the highway and for the forts that are built along the route."

"Will the Indians agree to that?" asked Pa.

"Nobody knows," said De Smet. "The government officials have asked for my help, to prevent great bloodshed. They know that I have some influence among the Indians and that I know different tribes."

"What will you do, Father?" asked Kathie.

"Help. I have to. Although I know that the Indians will be wronged again. They were promised this land and now they have to leave again or accept great losses."

"Do you know places where gold could be found?" asked Ma.

"Yes, I know some. But I would never reveal them."

They were golden days. Even the weather played along; there was only sunshine every day. During the day they worked outdoors, Ma and Kathie also in the house, and in the evenings they sat comfortably together. De Smet talked about his travels, and he was particularly fond of the Missouri, its beautiful shores, nature, wildlife, and flora. He described it in such detail that it seemed to Pa and Ma and Kathie as if they were witnessing everything. They sailed with him in the boat and watched the banks glide by, they saw waterfowl rising from the reeds, they were frightened with him when a group of Indians stood on the shore and forced him and his people to land. You didn't know whether it was friend or foe. When the Indians saw the cross that he had hung around his neck, they were quickly reassured and welcomed him with joy. Sometimes he had to go to their camp, which delayed the journey a lot and messed up his schedule, but he always knew how to take advantage of the opportunity to talk about God and baptize children in order to "open the way to heaven" for them, as he said. Friendships were formed, and the Indians are loyal friends.

"When I travel up the Missouri," he told them once, "I sometimes hear all the languages of the world, see people of all colors: white, black, yellow, red, and all the shades in between. The passengers disembark where they wish, to start farms, build mills, small towns and villages pop up as if by magic, on both sides of the river."

"Is the landscape beautiful?" asked Kathi.

"Very much so. There is everything you can imagine: boulders, plains with bushes and trees; oak, walnut, maple, poplars. There is also dogwood, which blooms white in spring and bears red berries in fall. Then there are wild cherries, mulberries, and much more.

But the banks of the river often break down, so the water is also quite muddy. Sandbanks and submerged trees are so common that you slowly get used to them and no longer think about the danger they pose. The boat can tip over or sink at any time, people and goods can disappear underneath, even animals, ..."

He hesitated, and Kathie felt that he had once had a bad experience and didn't want to talk about it.

"When we travel through the land, we sometimes see lonely burial grounds of Indians. These are certainly high-ranking members because the graves have been made very carefully. The body is erect, in a sitting position in a small cabin made of braided twigs to keep the wolves away. The dead man's face is dyed red, and the body is painted with war symbols. Next to it are food, dried meat, tobacco, powder and lead, rifle, bow, and arrows. For a few years, the families come back every spring and bring new dishes. They believe that the soul of the deceased remains close to the body for a long time, and only then rises into the land of the soul."

"That is beautiful," said Kathie. Ma looked doubtful. "Isn't it more beautiful when the soul detaches itself from the body and at the same moment goes to heaven and is received there by God, by Jesus, Mary and our angels?"

"It's still beautiful," insisted Kathie. De Smet gave her a warm look.

"I like it, too. But it is heathen. We just don't believe that. Their burial customs also throw a significant light on the Indians. Their cohesion, their love for their family. This is also one of the reasons for the hatred that the Indians harbor towards the whites. The government keeps putting them in other places that are not only barren, but that also take them far away from the burial places of their ancestors."

"What prevents them from accepting our faith?" asked Ma. "It is a faith of love, without hatred and revenge. If they would gradually accept it …"

"A lot hinders them," said De Smet. "First of all, the traditional. The magical-mythical. But then also very specific things like drinking. The boats keep bringing huge quantities of alcohol. It is incomprehensible, and really terrible, how much the Indians have become attached to drinking. And then they become cruel, even towards members of their own family, who are so important to them in their normal state. They behave like barbarians. I can't tell you some of the things I have seen. Nor would I want to."

"You see?" said Ma, "they are savages!"

"And where do they get the alcohol from?" asked De Smet, "from the whites, they wouldn't have it otherwise."

"Are they even interested in our faith?" asked Pa.

"Yes," said De Smet, "I have been in situations that were so heartwarming and promising for me that I thought to myself: 'Now I have them! They will find our wonderful faith inspiring!' Imagine we are sitting in the meadow, surrounded by flowers, and I tell them stories from the Holy Scriptures, about the Creation, the Flood, Noah's Arc. Of course, they love that. When I sit with the, I have the feeling that I am sitting with children. We laugh and joke and eat … although sometimes what I have to eat is more of a punishment!"

"Innocent? Like children?" Ma asked wide-eyed. "They can get so angry!"

"So can we," said De Smet seriously.

Kathie knew that this time of intimate fellowship would not last forever, and one day the time had come: the hour of farewell had arrived. It was a bright, clear fall day when he led his Lizette out of the stable. He had stowed his belongings in his travel bag, including some provisions from Ma. He shook hands with everyone. They felt that he was also suffering from the pain of separation.

"Say a prayer for us, Father," Ma said, moved. He thought for a moment, and then said "I want to say goodbye with a poem that an Indian addressed to the Great Spirit. And it is quite fitting for us whites, too:

>'I am a feather on the bright sky
>I am the blue horse that runs in the plain
>I am the fish that rolls, shining, in the water
>I am the shadow that follows a child
>I am the evening light, the luster of meadows
>I am an eagle playing with the wind
>I am the roaring of the rain
>I am the glitter on the crust of the snow
>I am the long track of the moon in a lake
>I am a flame of four colors
>I am an angle of geese in the winter sky
>I am the whole dream of these things
>You see, I am alive, I am alive
>I stand in good relation to the earth
>I stand in good relation to the gods
>I stand in good relation to all that is beautiful'

That is what the Indians feel when they think of the Great Spirit. It is praise for creation, and I believe we can also feel that way."

He turned his horse around and rode away. He rode down the Indian path and disappeared behind the hill. Pa shrugged his shoulders and went into the house. Ma followed him in silence. She began to prepare their evening meal. Pa lit his pipe and said:

"It was nice to have someone here, who is prepared to tackle anything. He sees everything, he can do everything; it was a pleasure to work with him. Our farm is perfect now. The fence has been straightened, the stable has been repaired, the damage to the roof caused by the storm has been fixed …"

"And the wonderful stories in the evenings!" said Ma. "We will miss him so much."

Kathie said nothing. She went up the ladder to her attic room, laid down on her bed and buried her face in her pillow. Then she went back downstairs and helped her parents. She would have more to do now.

New Settlers

One day, Ma sent Kathie to the Whites, to reconnect. She sent her schoolbooks along with her, in the hope that Mrs. White would find some time for the girls and teach them a little. Everyone was very pleased when Kathie arrived and even she was surprised by how happy she was to see this family once again. Mrs. White hugged her as if she didn't want to let go, and she was almost buried in her huge, soft hug. She was like a second mother. She brought pie and raspberry cordial, made from the raspberries she had gathered in the valley the previous year and made into juice. The children devoured the pie and Mrs. White asked wistfully whether her parents might also have time to stop by one time. Of course, she was particularly interested in Ma, with whom she could indulge in a little "girl's talk". She had received the latest issue of the "Godey's Lady's Book", that she wanted to read together with Ma – Kathie knew, however, that Ma would not be very interested in that, and she also had a catalog from which they could order crockery and other useful things, and they could chat about practical things, too; how to master the difficulties of a prairie household, and much more.

"Ma will come soon," said Kathie confidently, as she knew that her mother would also love to chat with Mrs. White. There was another married couple, Mr. and Mrs. Wilder, who had a baby, they could also be invited. All three men were farmers, and so they certainly had a lot in common, and much to talk about. Of course, the dominant topic of conversation was the Indians.

They finally managed it at Christmastime. All the families came together. Two bachelors were living just two miles further in a quarry; they had bought two plots of land, or rather "staked their claim," and built their house right on the boundary between the plots. Half the house stood on each of the plots of land. So, they lived in one house, but on two plots of land. They were two funny men, but anything but farmers. They were hunters and trappers and were often away from home for days.

"Let's just hope the Indians don't set fire to their place one day when they are gone," Pa had once said thoughtfully.

"Well, they could," said Mr. White, "but I don't think that would bother them too much. They love to take risks. They would simply re-build their cabin. They're often in towns, where there's something going on; Oswego, Abilene, Independence. They're not like us, not attached to the place, so to speak, and wanting to build something."

"But it would still be good if they would stay," said Pa, "the more of us there are, ..." He stopped suddenly and looked at Kathie.

"And what do you wish for, Kathie?" he said.

"I wish for a small community, a store, a school, a church ... that other people would also settle here, because they think they could have a good life here. And friendship with the Indians, who live near here and whose land we took."

Mrs. White looked worried.

"You don't seriously think that these people, whose land we have taken, could ever feel anything like friendship towards us, do you?"

"We didn't know it was their land," said Kathie. "If we could get in contact with them and explain it to them, then they would understand."

"Even if we were in contact with them – God forbid – we don't speak their language! How could we speak with them or explain anything to them?"

"De Smet could do it," said Kathie, "he can speak the Indian languages."

"But he is not here," said Mr. White, "and he has far more important things to do!"

"I can say what I would wish for!" said Kathie. "I wish we would have a small church, and a few times a year Father De Smet would come and celebrate mass. I know it isn't possible, and that he travels for months, but that is what I wish for. And I may say that. And I also know that it would be enough for him.

It would be important enough to him. And he would be like a magnet that would attract people. And our community would grow and grow."

"Those are nice thoughts, Kathie," Ma said warmly, "and I know just what you mean. But we can't see into the future. Who knows what may come."

In the meantime, Mrs. White and the girls had been busy in the kitchen and now they came out to to serve the guests. There was bread and ham, eggs, potatoes, and small, spicy pickles. There were also hot, brown cakes with maple syrup and stewed fruit made from dried fruits. There was tea, coffee, and fresh water to drink.

"I wish we could go down to the river again and pick berries," said Billie, wistfully. "Then Ma could use them to make her delicious juice."

"That's not possible at the moment," said Mr. White. "And the way I see it, that won't be changing any time soon."

"And when will it change?" she asked. Mr. White and Pa looked at each other.

"We just don't know," said Pa, "we are living in times of great uncertainty."

"What does De Smet say about all this?" Mr. White said later, when the dishes were done, and everyone was sat around comfortably.

"He's not clear about the connections either," said Pa. "There are different tribes, and in the different tribes, there are different people. Some hate and loathe the whites, others want to live in peace with them, probably also because they suspect that resistance would only hasten their downfall. He was invited to a council, in Laramie. There, the whites want to negotiate with the chiefs of the various tribes. And they need De Smet for that, so that they can achieve a good result. He knows the Indians like no other. He can mediate between the different tribes. That's worth more than a force of arms."

"How do you think he will mediate?"

"He wants to remind them of their joint origins. They have to stand together and defend their joint interests. He wants to get them far enough that they recognize America's right to build roads and military posts in their territory."

"The 'right'?" asked Kathie with a soft defensiveness in her voice.

"I know what you mean," said Pa. "But he must and will try if he wants to help them. But he also wants to make them pay for all the losses and damage they have caused the whites."

Mr. White looked skeptical.

"Of course, the Indians will also get something out of it," said Pa, "otherwise it wouldn't work at all. The Indians would receive quite a lot of money for fifty years, and they could use that for whatever they wish."

"For alcohol," said Mrs. White, "that's all they're interested in. And then, when they get into that state, to scalp a few white people on the side. After all, they can't think of anything else!"

"Come now, Bessie!" said Mr. White.

"Well, it's true," Kathie heard herself say, although she didn't really want to say it, "he once said that Indians get completely out of control if they get their hands on alcohol. And how do they get their hands on alcohol? From the whites. They often pay for their beautiful hides with alcohol."

"Well, we'll just have to wait and see what happens," said Pa. "He will do his best to remain neutral. And he can do that. I'm just curious to whether that will affect our tiny little corner of the world."

"Oh, it will," said Mr. White, "the Indians are everywhere. And Independence is a major center."

The Council of Laramie

The days passed and became weeks then months. Helping with housework, school with Mrs. White, celebrations and holidays, trips to Independence, to get a taste of the 'city air'. Pa's Farm had grown a little larger. Jack and Jim, the two bachelors, often came around to help Pa and keep in contact. They always brought them news from the 'big, wide world', or at least this tiny part of the world where they found themselves.

Now and then they would hear something about De Smet, about the preparations for the Indian meeting in Fort Laramie, but they didn't know much either, preferring to hang out in the saloons of Abilene and Oswego. Pa, however, got his news from Irwin's Grocery in Independence, which was occasionally frequented by Indians who were peaceful and traveled far and wide.

"The meeting will take place soon," said Pa one evening, when he returned from Independence laden down with lots of good things. Ma was glad of crackers, pickles, tea, brown and white sugar, flour, and many things that made life on a lonely farm pleasant. He talked about how cozy it had been at Irwin's Grocery.

"Some were playing cards, others a game of dice, and most were talking about things concerning life here with us. The Indians don't seem to be a problem at the moment."

"But for how long," asked Ma, who had just unrolled a bale of fabric that Pa had brought her. They were to be new curtains.

"Is there any news of De Smet?" asked Kathie quietly.

"Yes," said Pa. "There's been news. Of course, everyone is talking about him. He's a famous man."

"But nothing specific?" asked Kathie.

"No. Just that he is traveling around, often thousands of miles, visiting with the Indians, consoling them, baptizing children, trying to bring about peace and reunite enemy tribes, teaching them about the Christian beliefs that open the gates to heaven and eternal life."

"Good," said Kathie, "that's good. At least we know that he's alive!"

"Yes," said Pa, "but he's living dangerously."

It was 1851. It was September, a golden fall day. Kathie stood in the doorway and watched as a covered wagon approached their land. That was a rarity here, so she stopped and asked herself whether there were perhaps people who wanted to stop by. But the wagon stopped a short distance away and a man jumped down. He wore a black cowl and someone inside the wagon passed his travelling bag down to him. Kathie stood frozen in amazement and joy. And then she began to run.

"Father De Smet! Father De Smet!" She came to a halt in front of him, out of breath. He took her in his arms.

"Kathie! My Kathie!" He hugged her tightly and then let her go.

"How are you? And your parents?"

"We're well!" she said and looked at him with a beaming face. "And now we're a thousand times better!"

Together they went into the house.

How astonished the parents were at their guest! "This can't be true, this can't be true!" said Pa over and over again, while Ma immediately ran to the stove to prepare something good. De Smet sat down on the bench near the window, where he had sat so many times before.

"Do you have anything to refresh a weary traveler?" he asked, winking as he knew that he would have a full plate in front of him in no time at all. He already knew Ma so well. And so it was: baked beans, bacon, eggs, and fresh bread. He tucked in with the same appetite they already knew he had. Kathie was so happy that she couldn't get a word out.

Then Pa brought out a great surprise: a bottle of wine! He had been to Irwin's Grocery a few days before and had bought it. "For a special occasion!" he had said. And of course, today was such an occasion!

After the meal, Pa poured; a large glass for De Smet, a smaller one for himself and Ma, and Kathie got some too. Everyone tasted it and admired the blood-red color in the glasses. Everyone felt so warm and comfortable. It was a happy evening.

"Have you been able to eat something good recently?" asked Kathie, who had managed to find her voice, in the meantime.

"Yes," said De Smet and winked at her. "It was dog."

"What?!" Kathie shouted, realizing in the same moment that a young girl shouldn't scream like that. But she loved dogs. "That can't be true," she said quietly.

"Yes, it is true," said De Smet, "the Indians eat dogs, it is very normal for them. And it tastes good. They cook them with herbs and different spices. At first, I didn't know that it was dog either and then I asked. It would have been a great insult to turn it down. And so, I had to eat it. – You love chickens too, but you eat them, too. Isn't that right?"

"Yes, Father," Kathie admitted, "that is right."

"Do you have time to tell us something?" asked Pa. "How are things coming on?"

"There was a great meeting, the Council of Laramie. There were 10,000 Indians there, from all the different tribes, and the Indians were promised compensation for the land that the whites had taken for the highway and the forts that have been built along the highways. I tried everything to get the chiefs to agree to these terms. I know that my influence on them is greater than the government's promises and threats.

The proposals were read out and explained point by point to the interpreters, who then went from group to group of the various tribes. I did everything humanly possible to convince them of the government's good intentions. And they followed my advice."

"You have done great things," said Pa.

"I would do anything for the Indians," said De Smet, "that is why I came to America in the first place. But I also want to help the whites. These fertile fields are just waiting to be cultivated. There is simply everything here for the farmer. Orchards and vineyards could be planted, the forests are inviting for woodcutters, flocks of domestic animals could roam freely here. But what will become of the Indians who have owned the land here since time immemorial? I think in all directions, and I can't find an answer."

"The Indians could go to school, integrate, and become part of society," said Pa.

"Yes, they could," said De Smet. "And to some extent they do. But then comes the decree that the tribe has to move on. It has happened more than once.

But it is also the case that the Indians love the nomadic life. It is simply in their blood. They are hunters and gatherers. Suddenly they want to move on. And the mission is deserted."

Kathie didn't want to hear any more of it. She could feel how much it bothered him.

"Will you tell us about your homeland?" she asked. "Where do you come from?" She could feel how this revitalized him. She had achieved her goal of moving his thoughts, which were weighing him down, away from his problems.

"I come from Belgium," he said, "from a good family. My father owned a shipyard there, which my brother has now taken over. I have brothers and sisters, nieces and nephews, whom I love very much. We write often. Since I came to America I have visited once or twice to see my family and to collect money for my missions. And – as much as I love to be in America – it is always very hard to say 'goodbye' to the family I leave behind."

"There must have been a great celebration back when you left," Ma said.

"No," said De Smet sadly, "there was not."

"There wasn't?"

"No. I left home in secret."

"But why, for heaven's sake?"

"I wouldn't have made it through the farewell," he said. "I felt the call of God, I wanted to leave, I wanted to become a missionary. But I wouldn't have been able to bear the unhappiness I brought upon my family. I would have ended up staying."

"Is your country beautiful?" asked Kathie, to distract him from his gloomy thoughts.

"Yes, it is beautiful," he said, "Forests, the sea, mountains, beautiful cities and rivers, fertile fields and gardens … Maybe I have that in the back of my mind somehow, and I want to transplant it here: Gardens, productive fields, big farms, happy pets ..." His voice softened.

"Let us sit a while in front of the house," said Pa. "Kathie, bring me my harmonica!" They gathered round and waited until night fell. Above them the sky was a dome with millions of stars and the wind blew around the bushes and the prairie grass. Pa played warm, heartfelt melodies. They didn't sing this time. They just listened to nature and the wonderful sounds of the harmonica.

Finally, said Ma thoughtfully, "I think it's time to go to bed."

"Yes," said De Smet and smiled to himself in that special way that Kathie loved so much. "I think so, too."

"You go on up now, I'll be right behind you."

"Yes," Kathie said and stood, knowing that the adults wanted a few more minutes alone.

He stayed for a few days and helped Pa wherever he could. There was always so much to do on a farm. In the evenings they sat together, and he told them all about his plans. The Council of Laramie was over, and he had poured all his strength and ideas into that. Would it be enough to keep the peace? And if it wasn't, what would become of his missions?

Sometimes they rode out a little into the beautiful countryside. De Smet saddled the horse, lifted Kathie up, and then seated himself in front of her. He took up the reins and turned the horse along the Indian path that stretched out into the prairie. They rode without a destination, and sometimes just let the horse decide where to go. The scent that rose from the grasses was overwhelming, small birds took flight, and tiny beetles climbed up the grass stalks swaying in the wind. There were butterflies and honeybees everywhere. Ground squirrels sat attentively and then disappeared into their burrows in a flash.

One day, De Smet turned the horse down into the hollow, where there was a small pond. He jumped down from the saddle and lifted Kathie down. They led Lizette to the large wild rose bush, and tied her reins, just like Kathie had done that time. The flowers had withered, and beautiful red fruits shone against the bright, blue sky.

He stretched out in the grass and Kathie lay down next to him.

"Why did you do that back then?" he asked her quietly. "Did you realize that you were playing with your life?"

"I did," said Kathie, "I knew it."

"Then why?"

"Because my life has no value, without you."

There was a long pause. He had closed his eyes, but he wasn't sleeping. He was thinking.

"Kathie, you know that I am bound. I feel a lot for you, but I can't let that happen."

"I'm not asking for anything and I'm not expecting anything," Kathie said bravely, "but I want you to live, to be happy, and to be able to see you once in a while."

For a long time, they simply lay next to each other and savored the feeling of togetherness, then he stood and helped Kathie to her feet.

"We have to get back," he said.

"Yes," said Kathie, "my parents will be waiting for us."

Back at home there was tea, fresh bread, and salted meat. Then De Smet went outside, as he often did. Far from the house he stood still and looked up at the night sky. He soaked up the landscape with all its colors, sounds, and scents. The sound of a night bird drifted up from the bottom of the valley: "Huitt! Kiwitt-Kiwitt!" He sank to his knees and said:

"Father! My God! My Creator, Lord of all life! There is no-one higher, and I will not allow a child to mean more to me than You!" Then he performed his evening prayers with great devotion, as he always did, and returned to the house strengthened.

The Murder of Marshal Tom Smith

The next day they received a surprise. When Kathie stood in the doorway. She saw two small points in the distance, growing larger as they drew nearer. It was two riders. Kathie was about to disappear back into the house when she recognized the pair. It was Jack and Jim, the two bachelors who lived on the other side of the hill. They halted their horses and dismounted and let the horses canter round in a small circle, to finish up the hot ride. Pa came out of the house and called:

"What's wrong? Has something happened?"

"Yes!" called Jack, completely out of breath.

"What is it?"

"A murder!" Ma also hurried out of the house. She had been preparing the evening meal and was wiping her hands on her apron.

"A murder?" she repeated, paralyzed with shock.

"Indians?"

"No," said Jim, who had now also drawn closer, "whites."

"What happened? And who has been murdered?"

"Tom Smith, the marshal from Abilene."

De Smet had just come in. He was very concerned.

"How could that happen?" he asked. "Do you know any more?"

"Yes," said Jack, "we heard it from some traders. It is unbelievable what happened."

"As far as I know, he has never touched a weapon," said De Smet.

"How do you know that? Did you know him?"

"Yes," said De Smet, "I knew him. And I suppose you could say he was a kind of idol for me, because he could beat his way out of the most dangerous situations, with his fists."

"And if the others ignored that?"

"They don't – or at least, they didn't until more recently," said De Smet. "Please tell me more about what happened. It is an unwritten law that you don't shoot at an unarmed man. That has always been the way, in the saloons, and out in the open. It was like a code of honor. He cleaned up the town, which was teeming with bandits, with an iron fist, so to speak. So, what happened? What went wrong?"

"Tom Smith heard about a shootout. There was a dead man on a farm just outside Abilene. Tom Smith and his deputies rode out there. It was an isolated farm. The murderers were holed up in the house and were firing warning shots. His deputies tried to warn him. But he said: 'I'll get them out!' He was so sure of himself. He went, alone and unprotected, just like he's always done. But one of the murderers fired a shot at him. Although he was hit, he went into the house. The second man was standing behind the door and knocked him out dead."

Everyone was silent. After a while, De Smet said, "A man, who always wanted the best! He did so much for Abilene! No crime went unpunished there. He was brave and just. What a terrible end!"

"Why did you come here to tell us this?" Pa asked. "Abilene is quite a ways from here!"

"The murderers are on the run," said Jack, "and no-one knows which direction they took. Often criminals on the run ride very far, looking for lonely farms where they won't be discovered, they stock up on provisions and then ride on, but not without ..." Ma gave Jack a sign and he immediately shut up. But Kathie would have liked to have heard more about it. She had realized how much she loved adventure. The story of the lonely, upstanding marshal, who had died while carrying out his duty, had moved her greatly.

"Are all marshals so selfless and good?" she asked quietly.

"No," said De Smet, who had managed to compose himself in the meantime.

"Often it is gunslingers and gamblers who become lawmen."
"But why?"

"That's just how it is," said De Smet, "the people of the borderlands often face a dilemma. Sometimes, when they look for a keeper of law and order they have to choose between a fellow citizen who is upstanding, but weak, or a newcomer with a dubious past. Who will stop at nothing. They often choose a known scoundrel as marshal because they think such a man would be better suited to dealing with people like himself."

Kathie looked at him in amazement. He knew everything there was to know about life, its beauty, but also its cruelty and harshness. And she thought: "I want to be just like him! And how lucky am I that I am able to know him!"

"Tell us more about your friend," she said quietly.

"What is there to say," De Smet said sadly. "He came from humble beginnings and had to fight his way out; simply to stay alive. He didn't think much of firearms.

When he was offered the post in Abilene, he decided not to rule the people with powder and lead, but with his fists. He banned the carrying of firearms in the town. Anyone who resisted was beaten. He settled fights, ran cardsharps out of town, caught killers and arrested rustlers. He was respected by friend and foe alike. His personal courage and fairness were famous everywhere."

"And still something went wrong," said Kathie sadly.

"Not necessarily," said De Smet, "his time had come. He is with God now. And he did so much good! And death came fast for him."

"We should pray for him," said Ma visibly upset.

"Yes, each one for himself," said De Smet and went outside. He didn't want anyone to see how moved he was.

It was silent for a few minutes, and everyone thought about brave Tom Smith, who had met his death in the line of duty.

Ma went to the hearth to fix something good for lunch. Pa and the boys sat in front of the house, to exchange news. Kathie didn't think she would be wanted there because she knew that the men would talk more freely than if a girl were sitting next to them and listening to them. She would hear about the most important things later on. And as Ma also didn't call on her to help – she didn't much feel like kitchen work anyway – she snuck quietly upstairs to her beloved attic room. She sat in her chair opposite the window, so she could watch the clouds rolling across the blue sky. The clouds moved on, too. Further on their way.

Kathie thought about what she had seen in her lifetime. She didn't know anything; she never went anywhere. Everything exciting she knew she had heard from adults or had read in book. The events of history, as well as the adventure stories, made it impossible not to feel the excitement and empathize with these heroes.

But what about her own life? She really wanted to see and experience whatever was going on out there, she wanted to experience the atmosphere of a saloon, watch the barkeeper as he poured whiskey, and the men playing poker in a smoky corner, be witness to someone catching another player cheating and drawing his revolver. She wanted to see a bar fight and how the saloon keeper threw someone out. She wanted to hear the piano tinkling and see wicked ladies, who took the men's money. She would also love to see a shootout, from a distance, of course.

The death of the brave Tom Smith had stirred all this up in her once again. And then she thought of De Smet and the adventurous life he led. He had survived all the dangers so far and he was not afraid. He always said, "I am in God's hands." And Kathie wasn't afraid either. She was also in God's hands.

She compared his life with that of the brave marshal. Tom Smith had only ever done good and had followed his conscience. And in the end he failed. What would happen in De Smet's life? She didn't dare to even think about it. Always surrounded by danger. She couldn't stand at his side. And there it was again: that feeling of unconsciousness she so often felt whenever she thought about him.

His ideals – would they perhaps also shatter one day? Someone who only wants what is good will end up empty-handed. She wished him a beautiful, happy, fulfilled life so much.

Where would De Smet's journey take him now? He had mentioned that he wanted to visit the enemy Sioux, who had not taken part in the first council. They no longer believed the promises of the white men. The government had asked him to accompany a military expedition. But he didn't want to do that. He thought that it would destroy all his influence with the Indians if he went with armed soldiers under the flag, which, to them, would be the symbol of the end of their people.

He said that the Indians had always regarded him as the bearer of the Word of the Great Spirit until now, and they were always friendly and attentive when he met them. If he were to present himself in the midst of the soldiers of the Great Chief in Washington, who was no longer their Great Father but their greatest enemy, it would put him in an unpleasant situation. The crucifix he wore around his neck would no longer be a passport for him in Indian country.

He had decided to travel of his own accord, without payment, although that would have been important for his missions.

Kathie would have loved to have seen an Indian village. With the tents, and how they were furnished. There were beautiful, magnificent tents, and small, miserable, dirty ones; that's what De Smet had told them. There was cooking, washing, handcrafts. The Indian women were very gifted artistically. They embroidered, worked with glass beads, and made clothing from wool and leather. The men liked to play when they weren't hunting; there were games with cards and dice and games of skill. They liked to gamble and would bet everything they owned.

Children were important. They were never alone. They were always with their family groups. Someone was always looking out for them.

As she sat there daydreaming, thinking about everything De Smet had ever told her, the smell of food drifted up to her. She was a little ashamed that she hadn't helped Ma to prepare the meal, especially as there was so much more to do today, but Ma hadn't asked her. Still, she got up and went down and asked Ma bravely:

"Do you need any help? I know I'm a little late in asking!"

"No," said Ma friendly and stroked her cheek. "I know you had other things to think about. You go on out to the others!"

At that moment, the men came in. De Smet was with them. Now they could all smell what there was to eat. It was fish.

"Take a seat at the table!" called Ma. The large table was covered with a red and white checked cloth. There was salt and pepper and also pickles in the middle of the table, and the cutlery had already been set out. There was a jug of water and glasses, and Kathie's conscience stirred again, because she at least could have done that for Ma.

Then Ma brought a large pie to the table, beaming. The pastry on top was brown and crispy.

"Fish pie!" Pa shouted happily. "We haven't had that in forever!"

"Fish pie!" shouted the two bachelors, "this is a feast! Is it for us?"

"For all of us!" said Ma.

"Now tuck in! It is my greatest pleasure when everyone enjoys it!" Ma shared out the pie and wanted to give De Smet the first piece, but he refused it.

"Serve our guests first; I'm almost part of the furniture!" So, Ma served everyone and De Smet insisted on having the last piece. It was a lot smaller than the others and he seemed very pleased with that.

"That will never fill you up," Ma said fearfully.

"Oh, yes!" he said cheerily. Kathie wasn't sure what it meant. She knew that he enjoyed his food. But then she realized.

"You don't like fish?" she asked quietly.

"No!" he whispered in reply.

"Me either," mumbled Kathie and they both laughed. They tried to hide it, but they couldn't keep it in and eventually the others noticed.

"What's going on?" asked Pa. "Let us all share in your merriment!"

"We were just both thinking the same thing," said De Smet, "and it made us laugh. It was nothing special. And somehow it was a compensation for all the sad things we experienced today."

The others thought so too.

Sheriffs and Gunslingers

While they were eating the conversation turned once again to marshals and sheriffs; how it could be that someone who had already broken the law several times could come to take up such a post.

"There are men," said De Smet, "who live from the fact that they handle their weapons faster and safer than others. They exert a power over their fellow citizens that is based solely on their revolvers. The Colt is their law. Those men are adventurers. The lawmen with the star on their chest as well as the outlaws. And the lines between them are fluid and change frequently. There are people who aren't cut out to lead a normal life. They just want to survive these times in which we live."

"But you can do that without resorting to gunfire," suggested Ma.

"Normally, yes. But there are people who were born into difficult circumstances. A broken family, the father, a drinker; debts, violence. The son tries to escape the situation. He becomes a gambler, he signs on as a cowboy, kills for the first time.

These people get caught up in the machinery. They meet criminals. They rob a bank for the first time, or hold up a stagecoach, and they see that it works.

Of course, the saloons are a breeding ground for crime. A cardsharp is shot, his friend avenges him – you can imagine how it ends." He stopped because Ma threw him a glance.

"No, I can't!" said Kathie beaming. "Please, tell us more stories! I want to know what is going on in the big, wide world!"

"I know!" De Smet said, warmly. "Maybe another time. It's enough for today, I think." Evening had fallen. Kathie followed him. He sat down on the bench outside and Kathie sat down next to him.

"I want to know how people, who come from a good family, can become so bad that they murder people and are hunted, kill more people, and then end up on the gallows. Surely they must understand at some point and mend their ways!"

"Sometimes that isn't possible," said De Smet. "Suppose a young man grows up on a farm. Life is hard and dull. Life on a small farm seems dull and boring to him.

He hears of settlers heading out west. He thinks there's a great adventure to be had there. He hears of buffalo hunts, Indian battles, discoveries of gold, and the building of the railway. He wants to get away … He wants to see all these wonderful things: he wants to feel, hear, smell, taste everything. He wants to get away from where he feels trapped. And then he takes a leap. He joins the buffalo hunters. He trades with the Indians. He can't gain a foothold. There's a gambling den in every town here in the West, no matter how small. He becomes a gambler. Cheating is a significant part of every such gambling hall. He soon realizes that things are not right here. And so, he also becomes a double-crosser. And during one such maneuver, he is shot. And his parents wait in vain for their son to return."

"But I don't want any of that," said Kathie, "I just want to know what life is like 'out there'! Then I would come right on back and appreciate everything twice and three times over. Every grass stalk would be three times as green, and every bush and every twig would have a golden sheen. I want to live here, and I am at home here. And I would never leave my parents. Each birdcall would be three times as loud …"

"For heaven's sake," said De Smet, "you would have to cover your ears all day long!" A flock of wild ducks flew over the house. They were heading towards the lake where they would spend the night.

"No," said Kathie, "only in the evening." They both had to laugh at that. The birdcalls and the laughter drew her parents out of the house.

"What is so funny?" asked Pa in astonishment, "haven't you ever heard wild ducks flying over our house?"

"It was something we were discussing before," said De Smet, "nothing to do with the flock of birds."

"Shall I get the harmonica?"

"Please do," said De Smet. "There is nothing better than rounding off an evening with music."

"And with a prayer," said Ma.

Pa played and they sang: "Thee will I love, my strength, my tower; Thee will I love, my hope, my joy …"

Kathie's eyes shone, and De Smet's eyes were moist too. They were together. They were like a family. De Smet stayed with them for another couple of days and then he was gone again. No-one could or would stop him.

Prayers – Christian and Heathen

The years passed. They didn't hear anything from De Smet, but Kathie knew that he was well. That's how connected she was to him inside. The fear that something had happened to him, and she didn't know, had long passed. She knew he would go his way and do the task that had been given to him by God: to work for the good of the Indians.

Beautiful days came, bright and full of sunshine. And there was always such a lot to do; in the house, in the fields, in the barn and at the edge of the forest, where the children finally dared once again to pick the raspberries and blackberries, so that their mothers could make juice. Stewed fruits and jams too, which were a welcome change in winter.

Kathie knew there was something large brewing. A meeting with the enemy Sioux. And he couldn't be stopped or disturbed. The lives of so many depended on him. The Indians' trust in him was boundless. He succeeded in many things. The only thing she and her family could do was to send him good thoughts and to accompany him with their prayers.

She knew many prayers, including children's prayers, prayers of guardian angels, and prayers to the Virgin Mary. But she often thought of the Indian prayer that De Smet had told her. They believed that nature was imbued with a mysterious divine power. Their word for the deity, the creative power, was "wakan tanka," could be translated as "great secret." It was every Indian's duty to honor the eternal and invisible every day. He respects the immortal in the animal, his brother. He spoke with the animal before he killed it: "Please forgive me, but we need your meat. My children are starving. We need your fur to make a warm blanket for the winter."

Kathie wanted to pray but couldn't think of anything. All the prayers she knew seemed pale and lifeless to her. And so, she prayed: "We thank the rivers and streams, which give us water. We thank the herbs, which give us their healing powers. We thank the wind, which moves the air and drives away disease. We thank the moon and the stars, which send us light when the sun has disappeared. Above all, we thank the Great Spirit, who unites all good and guide everything to the good of His children."

She started. This was an Indian prayer, heathen! And she was a Christian! She prayed for a catholic missionary! And yet this prayer made her feel so warm, and she knew he would like it.

She wanted to turn her thoughts to Christian prayers, but all she could remember were fragments. After the Lord's Prayer and Hail Mary she remembered; "God, it is you in whom I trust. Through the life, death, and resurrection of Your son, you renewed the world ... how did it go on? ... so, I expect, for me and everyone, forgiveness, salvation, and future glory..." No, that wasn't it.

Suddenly she remembered: "Praise be you, my Lord! Through Brothers Wind and Air, and fair and stormy, all weather's mood, by which You cherish all that You have made!" That was a Christian prayer! A great saint had prayed it. And how similar his faith was to the Indian faith!

De Smet had also told her about the "holy circle of the Indians." He said: "It does not allow one to stand above the other. And in Christianity it says: 'You are not to be called 'Rabbi,' for you have one Teacher and you are all brothers.'

But we should not serve money – the idol Mammon – which the Indians do not like to deal with.

The Indians consider it impolite to show off one's knowledge. And it's the same with us. It is foolishness. True knowledge will be revealed to the simple.

To the weak, the small, and the afflicted, and to the last in line, he gives the Good News first; and let the strong bear the weak. This is part of Indian decency, and it is also a basic value in the Indian community."

So many similarities, but so many differences! How did De Smet deal with it? She hoped that she would get the chance to talk to him about it.

Encounter with the Indians

Time passed and not a lot happened. It seemed that the Indian threat had passed, for the time being, at least. A small group had formed around the White family, new settlers, celebrations in the houses, and even dancing. The two bachelors often came and Kathie suspected, that one of them was courting Billie. It would be nice if families grew here. It would be so nice if a small community would grow here. A small, solid, good community. With a church at its center.

On a warm afternoon in fall, everyone was sitting in Mrs. White's parlor. After coffee and cake the ladies read "Godey's Lady's Book" and considered what they could buy. There was a catalog, from which things could be ordered. Plates, bowls, cups, and everything you could need in a household. There were also catalogs from which you could order plants, trees even; but that was a matter for the men.

"I would so love to plant cottonwoods around the house, it would provide shade and slow the wind. What do you think, Tom?"

"I'm not sure if we should do that," he said. "We may have to up and leave at any time – very suddenly ..." Pa threw a warning glance towards the children.

"They are not children anymore," said Tom, "and they are ready to share our worries. Suppose we planted cottonwoods around our place. The Indians would see it."

"But they are not even here!" Pa interjected.

"They are here. We just don't see them. And they would understand that we were settling here permanently and making ourselves at home. On their land. My advice would be: we keep quiet. Add nothing to our properties. Of course, you can buy household goods, but they would be left behind if we had to leave the valley in the middle of the night – for some reason ..." Ma and Mrs. White had stopped reading their "Godey's Lady's Book." Ma nodded.

"That is what I think, too. We must not put anything at risk; don't risk anything."

"When will there be an end to this? It has been going on for years!"

"When we know that the Indians will accept the white man here. There will be a great meeting of the Indians, soon."

"And who would tell us what comes of it?"

"De Smet," said Kathie.

The following winter was hard and cruel; the coldest winter that Kathie had ever known. There was wind and snow and always a few clear days in between that Pa used to see to the animals and fix one thing or another. When he was gone for long, Kathie noticed how Ma would anxiously look up at the sky to see whether the black clouds were building again. He had tied a rope between the barn and the house because the snowstorms came on so quickly that you could lose your orientation.

One time it became so dark in the house, and Ma jumped up to open the door. Right at that minute, Pa came in and dropped a pile of wood onto the floor. At the same time, the storm broke out outside, lightening flashed, thunder crashed, and the snow pelted the house.

"Thank goodness, that was close," he said, and sat down next to the oven, breathlessly. The house seemed to rattle and shake. And then it came again, the knocking and the shout.

Kathie jumped up.

"What was that?" she shouted.

"Nothing," said Pa, "calm down. It's just the wind. It's shaking our house, but it can't damage it."

"And that shout?"

"Is also the wind. You should know that by now."

"Could it be a puma?"

"No. Those animals are too clever. They stay well-hidden during such weather, where they are protected from the wind."

"Do you remember all those years ago," said Kathie hesitantly, "when someone sought shelter with us in winter. The weather was similar to today."

"I know what you're thinking," Ma said warmly, and laid a hand on Kathie's shoulder. "But he is cleverer than a puma. He knows how to protect himself. He is bold, foolhardy; that is true. But he is not crazy."

"I am sure he's sitting in his warm room in St. Louis," said Pa. "He has a lot to think about and plan. He might even have time to deal with that herbarium of his, which is so important to him. And he will be writing his travel reports. Above all, he has to plan how he can influence the Indian meeting this year. A lot has been entrusted to him. He wants to do it all without the help of the government."

"Why doesn't he want the government's help? Why does he always want to do everything alone?" asked Ma.

"He has his reasons," said Pa. "He doesn't want to be the Washington president's messenger. He is no longer the "Great Father" of the Indians, but their enemy. They want him to tell the Indians that they will be wiped out if they continue to be hostile towards the white people."

"He can't do that. He won't be able to do that," said Kathie.

"He'll find his own words for it," said Pa.

Spring passed, the council of Laramie had taken place in summer; the meeting with the Sioux, and now fall came to the country. The prairie had become yellow, crossed with streaks of red sumac. On the horizon, the trees darkened, but were also slowly changing color: red, yellow, and brown. Flocks of wild geese rose up from the bottom of the valley, in formation for their migration further south.

Although Kathie did not worry about him, she longed to hear whether he had been successful. Whether it had been worth all his effort. Whether he had succeeded in helping the government to avoid further bloodshed.

And one day came a hint from God. Indians came riding up to the house. Pa, Ma, and Kathie had not seen any Indians in so long, that they simply stood frozen, rotted to the spot. They didn't know what it meant. They simply stood there and waited for them. There wouldn't have been time for Pa to get his rifle from behind the door, but he hadn't even thought about it. They would just have to let whatever happen.

The Indians came up from the bottom of the valley and rode along the old Indian path. They were twenty young men, in a parade, with rich feather headdresses, beautiful leggings and beaded moccasins. Their horses were not saddled or reined and obeyed the thigh pressure of their riders. Their manes flew in the wind and their eyes glistened. The first of the Indians – most likely the chief – lifted his hand and greeted them. And then they rode on past the house, along the path, and disappeared behind the hill.

"What was that?" groaned Ma. She was shaking from head to toe and was rooted to the spot.

"What was that?" asked Pa, "That was Indians."

"John, please, spare me your japes! What does it mean?"

"Well, it is definitely a good sign," said Pa, "otherwise the chief wouldn't have greeted us. Seems like the council of Laramie has borne fruit. I hope we'll find out more soon."

"I hope so too," said Kathie. "I hope with all my heart."

The Meeting with Sitting Bull

Another year passed before they learned any more. One day, when Kathie came home, she saw a lonely, black figure sitting on the bench in front of the house. She could hardly believe her eyes. She began to run. De Smet stood. He walked towards her. They hugged. His hair had grown grayer, but his beautiful blue eyes shone like always. Neither of them knew what to say. It didn't occur to her to ask him where he had suddenly come from. It was as if he had fallen from heaven just for her.

"How are you, Father?" asked Kathie.

"Good," said De Smet, and a shadow fell across his face. "And you? All of you?"

"Also good!" Kathie said bravely. "We have almost become a kind of community. Mrs. White teaches us. Mr. White has a small store. But what we are missing, of course –" she stopped.

"What is it?" he asked.

"A church. No town is complete without a church."

"No," said De Smet, "of course not."

"We could build one, of course," said Kathie, "but we don't have a priest, to hold mass for us."

"No," said De Smet. He looked down at the ground. Kathie didn't know what he was thinking. To cheer him up, she said:

"But I do have some news for you! We saw Indians!"

"Oh?" he said and smiled a little. "Well, that is truly a wonder in Indian country!"

"It is in this case," said Kathie, "we haven't seen a single Indian in years!"

"And how were they?" asked De Smet.

"Friendly," said Kathie, "and the chief even greeted us!"

"That is a good sign," said De Smet.

"That's what Pa said, too."

"I heard that the Council of Laramie is over now?" Kathie said carefully because she didn't want him to grow tired of her questions.

"Yes," he said bluntly. "I'll tell you about it later." She could tell that he needed a rest. He leaned his head back against the wooden wall and closed his eyes. She sat down next to him in silence.

Sometime later, Ma and Pa came home from the White's store. Kathie could tell that De Smet was pleased about the warm welcome he received.

"It's a marvel, such a store," said Pa proudly, and lifted the basket with the produce down from the wagon. "Now, at least, we can cater to you properly!"

They all went into the house and Ma showed off her purchases. "What would you like to eat tonight? Eggs with bacon and bread, pie, bean soup …"

"Whatever you serve is delicious," said De Smet. "I'll leave it up to you."

After supper, Ma set about making everybody comfortable. She shook out the red checked cushions by their corners and put the petrol lamp on the table to cast its warm light. Then she brought small plates with crackers and cubes of brown sugar and placed a large pot of scented tea on the table. Once she had served everyone, she leaned back expectantly.

"Do you know what I heard today?" asked Pa, to get the conversation started.

"What?" asked De Smet.

"They're going to build a small hotel next to the White's store! And they're planning a forge, too. When travelers come, either by horse or by wagon, and they need a blacksmith, they can buy their provisions and spend the night here as well!" Kathie was pleased to hear that, but she was more excited to hear De Smet's report.

"Was the Council of Laramie a success?" she asked once again, carefully.

"Yes, it was," said De Smet.

"And was your stay dangerous?" asked Ma.

"No," he said, "the stay itself wasn't, but the journey there was. The Secretary of the Interior and the Commissioner for Indian Affairs had asked me to propose peace to the Sioux, as an envoy of the government. I was supposed to travel together with the government officers, and they promised me a great reward.

But I was troubled. I didn't want to come as the "White Father's" messenger because he is now their enemy. I wanted to make the journey alone and at my own cost, although I could truly use the money for my missions. I rode out with a small group of friends. We traveled through the badlands, a plateau furrowed by huge canyons.

When we drew near to the enemy Sioux camp, I sent out four deputies. I gave them tobacco. Sending tobacco is always an invitation to discuss important matters. And then we waited, with great tension, of course. A few days later, riders appeared on the horizon: the scouts accompanied by eighteen enemy warriors. One of them said to me:

"Black Robe, we accept your tobacco. Chiefs and warriors await your visit. You are the only white person allowed to enter the camp."

The camp was another three days' ride away, at the estuary of Powder River. One day I saw a few hundred horsemen charging towards me from a hill. I took out my peace flag, which had the name of Jesus on one side and the image of the Mother of God surrounded by golden stars on the other. The Indians, who were charging towards me, suddenly pulled up. They were taken aback. At first they thought it was the star-spangled banner they hated so much. Four chiefs then approached and circled the flag. Then they realized their mistake, shook my hand, and gave the others a sign to approach. We then moved into the camp together.

I was assigned a large, beautiful hut in the village. Over the next few days, warriors always stood as a guard of honor in front of it. The next day, the Grand Council was convened to hear the United States' proposals.

The Great Council was opened with singing and dancing by the warriors. Then the eldest of the chiefs lit the peace pipe, offered it to the Great Spirit, the sun, the earth and the four points of the compass, and then passed it around.

And finally Sitting Bull, the most famous of all the chiefs, spoke to me:

"Speak, Black Robe! Our ears are open for all your words."

First, I raised my hands to the heavens and asked the Great Spirit for light and assistance. Then I explained to them why I had come. I told them of the danger threatening the red race, and described the horrors of a bloody, deciding battle. I promised them that the Great Father wished to treat the Indians with kindness. To replace the areas occupied by settlers, food and clothing would be delivered in abundance, also agricultural tools, and pets. The Great Father in Washington also offers them the opportunity to continue their education through schools and the learning of trades, and all this without giving up land.

After a short consultation, Sitting Bull rose and said to me: 'Black Robe has made a long journey to come to us. His presence in our midst fills us with joy. All the words he has spoken are wise, good, and full of truth. But our hearts bleed. They have received a thousand wounds. All these wounds are still open.

Against our will, the whites cut through our territory with their great roads, build fortresses and plant their guns there. They kill our game, even more than they need, are cruel to our people, mistreat and kill them on the slightest occasion. They cut down our forests, despite our objections, and without compensation. This is our land, and we are determined not to give up a single foot of it. This is where our fathers were born and died. This is also where we want to be buried.

You, messenger of peace, give us hope for a better future despite everything. Well, so be it! Let us hope! Let us spread a blanket over the past! Some of our warriors will accompany you to Fort Rice to hear the Great Father's proposals. If they are acceptable, peace shall be made."

"That was a wonderful speech!" Pa said, moved.

"Yes, it was," said De Smet, "the Indians are great speakers; Sitting Bull is especially known for it. At meetings where whites are also present, he always drives his opponents into a corner with his arguments, so that occasionally people try not to let him have his say at all, because they are simply no match for him."

"And they are Indians," Ma said, shaking her head. "Who would have thought it."

"And how did it all end?" asked Kathie.

"There was a large meeting in Fort Rice, with over 50,000 Indians in attendance. Sitting Bull set three conditions for peace: the whites must give up their forts, they must no longer demand land, they must spare the trees more, especially the oaks.

The generals made a solemn promise to the Indians that if they laid down their arms, the government would recognize their rights, provide for their livelihood, and treat them as friends.

"So, peace with the Sioux is all thanks to you," Pa said finally, "the endlessly long journey, in constant danger of being captured and scalped by the Indians ... bloodshed was prevented ... does the government even realize what it is you did?"

"Yes," said De Smet slowly after a few moments. "I think they do."

One day, when Kathie came home, she saw De Smet sitting alone on the bench. He hadn't accompanied them today. He was so lost in his thoughts, that he didn't notice Kathie until she was standing in front of him. He wanted to stand, but Kathie simply said: "Please, don't get up on my account. I will sit beside you."

She sat down next to him and looked at him.

"Father De Smet, are you worried? What torments you? Everything has turned out so well!"

For a long time, he said nothing.

"Everything went well at the beginning. But then things happened that I wouldn't have thought possible."

"What happened?" Kathie asked quietly.

"A short time later, the President turned to Protestantism. A Protestant was elected Chairman of Indian Affairs. Then the Indian missions were taken out of the hands of the Catholic Church and handed over to Protestant sects. Despite the constitutional freedom of religion, despite the objections of the Indians, who demanded their Black Robes and no other people, the Indians were suddenly handed over to other denominations. It even came to the point where Catholic missionaries were forbidden to even visit their former missions."

"The missionaries who founded these missions at great personal risk and danger to their lives are forbidden to enter them?" said Kathie, stunned with astonishment.

"Yes," said De Smet, sadly. "That's politics. And the Indians put up a fierce fight against the Protestants."

"Why though?" asked Kathie.

"It is families that are coming. A pastor has a family. The Jesuit has none. The Indians are his family. They want him to look after them – and only him, without any attachments. Now they could leave the missions. They are disappointed. They become estranged from the Christian faith again and begin to adhere to their pagan practices."

"What can be done?" asked Kathie.

"There is something that I have already done. I have handed in my resignation. As a procurator, and as a university lecturer."

"Good," Kathie said fiercely. "You are known throughout the land. The seed has been sown. Whether it will sprout is up to God."

"You are right, Kathie," he said, "but now one of my greatest wishes can never be fulfilled. I wanted to found a mission for the Sioux. Now I won't be able to."

He turned to her, and she saw that there were tears in his eyes.

"Don't be afraid, Kathie," he said quietly, "I weep easily." She jumped to her feet. She grabbed hold of his hands and held them tight. They were rough and worn. Then she pulled his head down to hers. He let it happen.

"I am suffering with you, Father," she said.

"Pierre," he said almost inaudibly.

"Pierre, may I counsel you?" she said gently. "You are burned out and tired. But you will regain your strength. Wherever you will be, wherever you will live, you will be a magnet! People will come to see you and you will proclaim the good news to them. You used to come to them, now they will come to you."

He looked up, and she saw the gleam in his eyes slowly returning.

"You are right," he said, "I won't let it get me down. There are still a few possibilities. There are many possibilities."

SITTING BULL.

A Community Forms

For the next few days, Pa and De Smet were back at work in the bottom of the valley, and Ma knew plenty of work to do to keep Kathie with her. Now she was beginning to feel sure that it was a surprise. She said nothing and figured that she would probably find out soon enough.

One day – it was Saturday – De Smet packed his bag. Ma was amazed.

"You'll be staying with us again tonight?"

"No," said De Smet, delightedly.

"But it is already so cold outside in the night!"

"That doesn't bother me," said De Smet. "I am tough."

Pa also made a sneaky face. And so, Kathie was sure that their strange behavior had something to do with the surprise she would hopefully soon find out about.

On Sunday morning, Kathie put on a nice dress. It was pale gray, adorned with small red flowers. Sunday was held in high esteem in the family, even if there was no mass to go to. They prayed together in the morning, at midday and in the evening, and Pa often read out a passage from the Bible and they discussed it. Kathie loved the Psalms the most, and of these, Psalm 23 was particularly close to her heart:

"The Lord is my shepherd; I shall not want. He maketh me to lie down in green pastures: he leadeth me beside the still waters. Yea, though I walk through the valley of the shadow of death, I will fear no evil: for thou art with me."

Ma always prepared something special for dinner, too. That morning everything happened with a strange haste, and Kathie saw Pa take the wagon out of the shed and harness the horse to it.

"Where are we going?" asked Kathie in astonishment.

"You'll see," Ma said secretively. Then she looked at Kathie. "Wouldn't you like to put on your best dress today?", she asked.

"This *is* my best dress," said Kathie.

"Don't you have one that is even more beautiful?"

Kathie had a dress, but it was only ever brought out for special occasions. It was dark blue and had a lace collar.

"You mean, I should wear the blue one?"

"Yes," Ma said, warmly, "wear that one. Today is just the day for it."

Ma was also dressed very festively in a brown wool robe with buttons that looked like ripe blackberries. Pa wore his Sunday jacket made of gray cloth.

They climbed into the wagon and drove down into the bottom of the valley. Kathie's heart was beating fast. What was going on? A birthday party with the White family? Where was De Smet? Had something been prepared for him that they could attend? She wasn't too excited because she sensed that Pa and Ma were looking forward to what was to come.

When they arrived at the Whites', they drove past the house. Pa steered the wagon into the large meadow behind the house and let them get out.

And then she saw it. She could hardly believe her eyes. A small building stood in front of her. Freshly carpentered, and the bright walls shone like pure gold. It had a tower at the top. It was a chapel!

All the people Kathie knew had gathered in front of the building. They were all standing there in eager anticipation. She also spotted a few faces she had never seen before. To the side, tied to a wooden post, she saw horses and two more carriages.

Suddenly, the doors opened and out walked – De Smet, with a bell in his hand. He rang and rang, and the murmuring fell silent.

"Please, come in for our first Holy Mass!" he said, with his warm voice.

They all entered in awe. The small church was so full that here was hardly room for everyone. Kathie stood at the very back and tried to control her movements. She knew what it meant. He had decided to stay.

"If things continue like this, he will soon have to expand," Pa whispered to Ma. Ma gave him a dismissive look. They were in the house of the Lord now, so such comments had to be silenced.

But Kathie knew that he was right. As soon as word got round that De Smet was here, people would come, in droves.

But then she tried to concentrate on the service. De Smet welcomed everyone in a very friendly manner, and then began the Holy Mass. For the sermon he chose the parable of the good shepherd:

"The one who does not enter by the door into the fold of the sheep, but climbs up some other way, he is a thief and a robber. But the one who enters by the door is a shepherd of the sheep. The sheep listen to his voice, and he calls his own sheep by name and leads them out. When he puts all his own sheep outside, he goes ahead of them, and the sheep will follow him because they know his voice. I am the good shepherd. The good shepherd lays down his life for the sheep. I know my own and my own know me."

Kathie knew why he had chosen this parable. She understood him so well.

After mass he was surrounded by so many people that Pa, Ma, and Kathie set out on their way home. That was fine with Kathie because she was in a daze and her knees were shaking. He had come to stay. She would be able to see him often. That was the great wish she had had for years. Not waiting, hoping, and fearing. She knew now where he was.

"What an extraordinary decision for him to make," said Ma. "Throwing everything away like that ..."

"He had had enough," said Pa. "They used him. And then they cut him off. The government has saved itself a lot of money. Major bloodshed has been avoided. – You just can't do something like that to someone as sensitive as him."

"Where will he live now?" asked Kathie, who had found her tongue once again in the meantime.

"Behind the church is a small extension; a kind of sacristy, and that's where he will sleep. A bed, a trunk; that's all he needs. Later, he will certainly add a few more things to make the room homely and cozy. A table, armchair, shelves for his books and writings."

"The settlement will thrive," said Ma, "I'm sure of that. Where there's a church, that's where people want to go. And with a priest like that to boot! I have to say, I can't contain my joy! The settlement will become a village, and then a small town with all the trimmings. And what will this little town be called?"

"DE SMET," said Kathie.

Epilogue

I got to know the beautiful town of DE SMET in South Dakota on a trip through America. There, I learned that Jean-Pierre De Smet was a famous missionary and friend of the Indians, who lived in the 19th century, a mediator between Indians and whites. I read a lot about him and tried to imagine his interesting life.

I would like to thank Kirstie Stuart-Hiess for the insightful translation.

The author

Brigitte Hoffmann-List was born in 1942 in Vienna. She studied German Studies and Early History at the University of Vienna. She is married with two daughters and lives, with her family, in Alland in Austria.

Previous publications include:

Publishing House: Edition Weinviertel
- Kleines Haus in Stadlau
- Ferien in Puchenstuben
- Das Geheimnis des Bruder Wolfhelm
- Aurelia – Kinderzeit in Carnuntum

Publishing House: Novum
- Mord im Kloster

novum PUBLISHER FOR NEW AUTHORS

The publisher

*He who stops
getting better
stops being good.*

This is the motto of novum publishing, and our focus is on finding new manuscripts, publishing them and offering long-term support to the authors.
Our publishing house was founded in 1997, and since then it has become THE expert for new authors and has won numerous awards.

Our editorial team will peruse each manuscript within a few weeks free of charge and without obligation.

You will find more information about
novum publishing and our books on the internet:

w w w . n o v u m p u b l i s h i n g . c o m